Understanding the Accuser

David Alsobrook

Sovereign World

Sovereign World Ltd
PO Box 777
Tonbridge
Kent
TN11 0ZS
England

ISBN 1 85240 238 5

This Sovereign World book is distributed in North America by Renew Books, a ministry of Gospel Light, Ventura, California, USA. For a free catalog of resources from Renew Books/Gospel Light, please contact your Christian supplier or call 1-800-4-GOSPEL.

The author may be contacted at:

Sure Word Ministries
PO Box 2305
Brentwood
TN 37024
USA

Typeset by CRB Associates, Reepham, Norfolk.
Printed in England by Clays Ltd, St Ives plc.

Contents

Chapter 1

Satan's Three Most Common Roles

Satan's diverse roles in attack

Our opponent, shrewd and subtle as he is (Genesis 3:1), is not confined to a single role or method of attack. A survey of the Scriptures reveals many kinds of operations against the people of God. If they successfully defeated the adversary in one of his schemes, he would come against them at a later time using another tactic. Jesus exhorted His followers to be as 'wise as serpents' and Matthew 10:16 shows that serpents do have a substantial level of intelligence.

As I studied the Word to find out more about the enemy of whom Paul said we should not be ignorant (1 Corinthians 2:11), I slowly became aware that Satan has three primary roles when attacking the believer. If one method does not succeed against a Christian, often another form of attack will. These three roles are:

1. The tempter,
2. The deceiver, and
3. The accuser.

The tempter

The first time we see Satan approaching mankind, he comes to our first parents, Adam and Eve, in his role as the tempter. The serpent tempted Eve by saying,

> *'Did God really say, "You must not eat from any tree in the garden?"'*
> (Genesis 3:1)

It was also in this role that the Lord Jesus encountered him in their first recorded confrontation:

> *'The tempter came to him and said, "If you are the Son of God, tell these stones to become bread."'*   (Matthew 4:3)

Evidently the early Christians were aware of this term 'tempter' and this tactic also, for Paul wrote,

> *'For this reason, when I could stand it no longer, I sent to find out about your faith. I was afraid that in some way the tempter might have tempted you and our efforts might have been useless.'*
> (1 Thessalonians 3:5)

The tempter's attacks are very real and sometimes successful in defeating a believer, but although temptation is the devil's **first** method of attack, it is actually the **weakest** of his three primary tactics. Jesus easily overcame this attack with single quotations of solitary sentences from the book of Deuteronomy. He did not have to use a lot of Scripture when the tempter came against Him. Single stabs with the sword of the Spirit actually defeated all three areas of temptation.

The deceiver

Far more believers are harmed by the devil when he comes as the deceiver than when he comes as the tempter. This is a higher realm of attack and much more subtle than the previous one. Paul was referring to this second method in 2 Corinthians 11:14–15 when, after shocking them with the fact that many of their apostles were false, he said,

> *'And no wonder, for Satan himself masquerades as an angel of light. It is not surprising, then, if his servants masquerade as servants of righteousness. Their end will be what their actions deserve.'*

Paul taught that even as false ministers appeared as true ministers, so also Satan can masquerade himself as a true angel of God. God is light and His angels are angels of light. Satan, in his actual state, is an angel of darkness. He is, however, able to disguise himself as an angel of light. I do not believe that Satan can actually change himself into an angel of light. I most definitely believe that Satan can and does **disguise himself** as an angel of light.

The purpose of coming to a person in the role of the deceiver is to trick that individual into accepting the false for the true. I personally know a number of ministers who have been deceived into great errors. Some of these have seared their consciences with moral error after a 'revelation from God' convinced them that we should have concubines today. Others have not brought such great shame as this upon the name of Christ, but have made their ministries invalid through teaching a distortion of Scriptures. The deceiver delights in distorting the truth of the Word and he shows this in Matthew 4:6 when he twists the clear meaning of Psalm 91:11–12. Jesus was not fooled by this trick. Even Satan can haphazardly quote (usually he misquotes) the Scriptures.

What then is our safeguard against this form of attack? After I sought the Lord earnestly along this line, He showed me. We have seen that a believer can overcome the attack of the tempter with a single confession of God's Word. Remember that Jesus used only one sentence to rebuke the tempter. However, a believer can overcome the deceiver only by studying the **whole counsel** of God's Word and rightly dividing the Word by interpreting Scripture **with** Scripture.

I have come to the conclusion that each Christian must work out his/her own salvation and not rely entirely upon the experience of others. Every person has their own set of problems and areas of weakness to overcome. He that sat upon the throne said,

> *'He who overcomes will inherit all this, and I will be his God and he will be my son.'* (Revelation 21:7)

The deceiver delights in taking a part of the Word and emphasising it to the exclusion of other parts of Scripture. Fortunately, many of us stay balanced in the Word sufficiently so that the deceiver's appearance as an angel of light does not fool us.

Most of you reading these words have known the presence of the tempter and the approach of the deceiver. When the enemy came to you in that first role, you were well aware of the temptation. When he approached you as the deceiver you were probably soon aware of his attack, although it was harder to discern.

We now come to the third, and I think, strongest form of attack. 'The devil' is the Greek word *diabolos* and means 'one who prosecutes as in a court room; a slanderer.' 'Satan' primarily means 'adversary' and also 'accuser – one who resists'. This role as the accuser is probably the hardest to discern and overcome. Often we ourselves unknowingly become tools with which the devil can work.

When Satan appears as the tempter, his presence is very obvious. When he comes as the deceiver, his presence is not always quite so obvious. However, when he comes as the accuser, we sometimes not only fail to recognise his voice, we may even mistake it for the voice of God! At that point we are deceived and will most likely give in to the temptation to pass carnal judgement on a fellow believer. Thus we are snared by all three of his traps.

How the accuser operates

There are three main ways that Satan operates as the accuser:

1. **Satan accuses the believer to God, and accuses God to the believer**. In the opening chapter of the book of Job we read that Satan accuses Job to God: *'"Does Job fear God for nothing?" Satan replied'* (Job 1:9). Twice the devil tells the Lord, *'...he will surely curse you to your face.'* (see Job 1:11; 2:5). Then Satan accuses God to Job (through his wife): *'His wife said to him, "Are you still holding on to your integrity? Curse God and die!"'* (Job 2:9).

2. **Satan accuses other Christians to a believer**. Sadly we often fail to realise this. We often look at another Christian and judge them at face value. Jesus referred to this as having an 'evil eye', which is grouped along with adultery, fornication and murder in Mark 7:19–24. It accounts for the great deal of suspicion, distrust, faultfinding and criticism that exists within the body of Christ.

3. **Satan accuses a believer to himself**. Even after a believer exercises true repentance over a sin and sincerely asks the Lord to forgive him, the accuser will attack with condemnation and guilt. Often I pray with Christians who have lived with guilt and burdens of condemnation for years and years. I am so happy to show them that it is Satan who condemns them and not God.

Throughout the rest of this book we will look at how to overcome these three attacks of the accuser in a more practical way.

Chapter 2

Overcoming Satan
When He Accuses Me to God

First of all we will look at how we should overcome Satan, the accuser – when he accuses me to God. Revelation 12:7–11 says this:

> *'And war broke out in heaven: Michael and his angels fought with the dragon; and the dragon and his angels fought, but they did not prevail, nor was a place found for them in heaven any longer.*
>
> *So the great dragon was cast out, that serpent of old, called the Devil and Satan, who deceives the whole world: he was cast to the earth, and his angels were cast out with him.*
>
> *Then I heard a loud voice saying in heaven, "Now salvation and strength, and the kingdom of our God, and the power of His Christ have come, for the accuser of our brethren, who accused them before our God day and night, has been cast down.*
>
> *"And they overcame him by the blood of the Lamb and by the word of their testimony, and they did not love their lives to the death." '*

The eleventh verse is well known since it is often quoted. We understand that the 'him' who is overcome by the blood and the word of testimony is Satan or the devil, but we are likely to overlook the role in which he is portrayed in this verse – that of the accuser.

We read here that John sees a great battle taking place in heaven. Some theologians teach that this Scripture has already been fulfilled. Those who interpret the book of Revelation solely on a spiritual level believe that this was completed when Jesus sprinkled His blood in the holy of holies after His resurrection.

Having studied Revelation from many points of view, I believe that chapter 12 is still in the future. John sees a time coming when Satan will no longer be allowed to accuse Christians before God.

Christ was crucified probably around AD 33 and this book was given to John around AD 95. Yet in Revelation 1:1 – over sixty years later – we read:

> *'The Revelation of Jesus Christ, which God gave Him to show His servants – **things which must shortly take place.'***

In other words, the book of Revelation concerns **things that are to come to pass**, and that was more than sixty years **after** Jesus had completed His work at Calvary.

Some people say the war between Satan and Michael took place at Calvary. If so, then why do the Christians overcome Satan by the blood of the Lamb in Revelation 12? It is evident they overcame the accuser after he had been cast down to earth. Verse 11 states that *'they did not love their lives to the death,'* and no disciple was martyred until **after** the sufferings of Christ had long been accomplished. So it couldn't have taken place just at Calvary. True, at Calvary the accuser was defeated for us, but the battle referred to in this passage has not come into effect yet. Michael and his angels have yet to war against Satan and his angels and cast them down from the heavenlies. We need to understand that Satan **still** has access to God.

But didn't Jesus say in Luke 10:18, *'I saw Satan fall like lightning from heaven*'? Satan was cast out of heaven in the past. He was cast out of heaven long before Calvary, when heaven was still his abode. Luke 10:18 validates Satan's loss of right to dwell in heaven. This occurred long before man had even drawn the breath of life.

The accuser has access to the throne

The book of Job, however, gives more insight into Satan's position. This book was written **after** man was created and **after** Satan had lost the right to dwell there. Chapter 1 verse 6 states:

> *'Now there was a day when the sons of God came to present themselves before the LORD, and Satan also came among them.*
> *And the LORD said to Satan, "From where do you come?" So Satan answered the LORD and said, "From going to and fro on the **earth*** [in other words he was not on the earth when he was saying these words], *and from walking back and forth on it." '*

1 Peter 5:8 tells us he still does this:

> *' . . . your adversary the devil walks about like a roaring lion, seeking whom he may devour.'*

This scene described in the book of Job was not on earth. This was in heaven, a familiar place to the devil. He had lived there for aeons and aeons. In all likelihood he was created there and later assigned to rule over the earth before the creation of man.

Satan comes to God, who asks him, 'Where do you come from?'

'From going to and fro in the earth,' Satan replies. Now this is after the fall of the anointed cherub, after the creation of man, after the time Jesus referred to when He said, *'I beheld Satan fall like lightning from heaven.'* Yet, whom is Satan standing before in Job 1 and 2? He is standing before Yahweh whose 'throne is in the heavens' (Psalm 103:19). This perplexed me for some time.

Satan was not in the earth, he was before God. God didn't come down to earth and say, 'You sons of God, you created angels, present yourselves before Me and Satan, come also.'

My problem was that Revelation 21:27 relates that no one may enter into the holy city who works abomination, or makes a lie, but only those who are written in the Lamb's book of life. How can he, then, enter into heaven and stand before a Holy God? Then I recalled the words: *'So then each of us shall give account of himself to God'* (Romans 14:12), and I saw it!

Satan has to give account of himself to God. Evidently this is something he does regularly, or periodically. In Job 1:6 we read,

> *'Now there was a day when the sons of God came to present themselves before the* Lord, *and Satan also came among them.'*

Compare that verse to Job 2:1:

> *'**Again** there was a day when the sons of God came to present themselves before the* Lord, *and Satan came also among them to present **himself** before the* Lord.*'*

So we see from these verses that Satan is periodically coming to present himself before God and to give an account of his recent actions on earth.

God's purpose in allowing Satan's entrance into heaven is to permit his rendering an account of his deeds, not to fellowship with him. And while Satan is reciting his activities, he takes advantage of the occasion to throw stones at the saints. Another common name for Satan is 'the devil.' Recall that the Greek word for 'the devil' is *diabolos*, which means 'prosecutor, slanderer, and accuser.' Standing before the Judge of all the earth to render an account of recent activities, *diabolos* takes advantage of the occasion to slander God's servants.

Observe Job 1:7: *'And the Lord said to Satan, "From where do you come?"'* After he answers the Lord, *'From going to and fro on the earth, and from walking back and forth on it,'* the Lord says to Satan, *'Have you considered My servant Job ... ?'* (You get on the enemy's target list when you serve the Lord!) Job was an upright man, one who feared God and avoided evil, so it should come as no surprise that Satan had a long list of accusations to make about him!

Jesus Christ, who was completely without sin, was inspected by the evil one in the same way. Jesus said,

> *' "I will no longer talk much with you, for the ruler of this world is coming, and he has nothing in me." '*
>
> (John 14:30)

Perhaps we could paraphrase this verse: 'The ruler of this age is coming to inspect Me, but he has no claim on Me.'

I'm so glad that when Satan inspected Jesus, he could not find one legal ground of evidence with which to accuse Him to the Father. Had Satan been able to find such ground, there would not have been a lamb without spot or blemish and we would have been hopeless and helpless.

When Satan accuses me to God he appeals to the legal holiness of God the Father. If at all possible, he will relate an actual fault in my life; if that is not possible, he will unjustly slander me before the throne. Were it not for Jesus, our Advocate at the Father's right hand, our adversary would gain the upper hand. God, because He demands holiness, would have to punish us. Thank God for an Advocate who is in the Father's favour!

In 2 Corinthians 2:10–11 Paul says he is not ignorant of Satan's devices.

> *'Now whom you forgive anything, I also forgive. For if indeed I have forgiven anything, I have forgiven that one for your sakes in the presence of Christ, lest Satan should take advantage of us; for we are not ignorant of his devices.'*

The word 'devices' means 'war plans' or 'war strategies.' In warfare our adversaries seek to spy out our weaknesses so that they may better attack us.

Returning to Job's story, Satan answers God with a tone of mean insinuation in his voice.

> *'So Satan answered the Lord and said, "Does Job fear God for nothing?"'* (Job 1:9)

His words implied that Job only served God because of the material blessings the Lord showered upon him.

God told Satan that he could strike everything Job had but not his life. After Satan's ravaging attack, in Job 2, we find that only Job's wife is left; his children are dead. Satan spared Job's wife because they were 'one flesh', and Satan had to obey and recognise that union.

Satan decides: 'If I can't get at Job directly, I can do it indirectly through his wife.'

> *'Then his wife said to him, "Do you still hold fast to your integrity? Curse God, and die!"'* (Job 2:9)

Satan can use others, even those closest to us, to get to us. In Matthew 16:23 Jesus quickly identifies the source of Peter's words as being the work of Satan. Satan's method here is to accuse God to Job through his wife's 'advice.'

Satan's two-fold attack is generally to accuse you before God, then accuse God to you. We see this in Genesis 3:12. After Adam had sinned, he accused God – he blamed his sinning on God. *'The woman whom you gave to be with me, she gave me of the tree, and I ate.'* Directly he was blaming his wife, but indirectly he was blaming God: 'The reason I'm in

16

all this trouble Lord, is because of the woman that **You** gave me. If **You** hadn't put me in this situation, I'd never have done this in the first place.'

Many Christians are bitter towards God. Suppose God answers ninety-seven of their prayers. Seemingly, three prayers don't obtain any answer. Satan is quick to say, 'Ah, look at God, He didn't fulfil His Word.' Satan accuses God to His people as well as accusing His people to God.

After Satan accused Job to God, he began to present the Lord his list about Job. In Job 1:10 five specific areas are highlighted regarding Satan's methods of 'believer inspection'. We have no reason to think that he has altered them through the millennia.

Satan inspects five things about Job and **you**:

1. **Satan inspected Job's conduct**. *'Have you not made an hedge around him?'* He knew all about Job and his personal life. He studied his habits. He listened to the words he spoke. He saw what he was like around the house. He knew how he conducted himself twenty-four hours a day. This thought is amplified in Psalm 119:23: *'Princes* [principalities] *also sit and speak against me, but your servant meditates on Your statues.'*

2. **Satan learned all about Job's family**. He knew Job's interpersonal relationships and *'all that he has on every side'* (Job 1:10).

3. **Satan made a detailed study of Job's possessions**. He knew how much silver and gold Job had, how many sheep, how many oxen, how many servants, etc.

4. **Satan watched Job's labour**. *'You have blessed the work of his hands.'* Satan knows what you are like at home or in your workplace. He knows how you respond to pressure at work. He is on the job when you are on the job! In the body of Christ, the phrase, 'the work of your hands' denotes ministry, and Satan knows about the work of your hands. He is forever trying to tie your hands and get you bound up so you can't

swing the sword, plough the field, sow the seed, and reap the harvest.
5. **Satan observed Job's social influence**. '... *his possessions have increased in the land'* (Job 1:10). The word 'possessions' means something more like 'social influence.' His social influence is increased in the land. Many times when the tempter overcomes Christians, it is relatively easy for them to get back into fellowship with God – that's not the hard part – but their testimony has been tarnished; the name of Christ has been marred. Restoring their influence with man takes much longer.

These are five areas that Satan inspected in Job, though it must be noted that Satan is **not** omnipresent and he is **not** omniscient. However, he will, given the opportunity, inspect us to see if he can find something in our lives to throw in God's face.

The accuser is muzzled by the advocate

In the book of Zechariah, chapter 3, we see a glimpse of what we are talking about. Zechariah prophesied during the post-exilic period after Israel had come out of the land of Babylon, where the Israelites had been in captivity, confusion and bondage for seventy years. Now they were back in Israel and God was blessing and prospering them.

Haggai, too, spoke to Israel near this time. His word to them was:

> *'Is it time for you yourselves to dwell in your paneled houses, and this temple to lie in ruins?'* (Haggai 1:4)

Decades previously Nebuchadnezzer's armies had come and led them away as captives. They had desecrated into a pile of rubble the beautiful temple built by Solomon.

Now, over a hundred years later, they are back in the land and have paneled houses to dwell in, but the temple is still a mound of ruin. God begins to challenge them to consider their ways and to rebuild His house.

Zerubbabel is the chief architect and master craftsman. God has a word for him:

> *'"...Not by might, nor by power, but by My Spirit," says the LORD of hosts.'* (Zechariah 4:6)

From the book of Nehemiah we know they were trying to rebuild the wall with a sword in one hand and a trowel in the other. Zerubbabel was to learn that the rebuilding of the temple was 'not by might, nor by power...' The words 'might' and 'power' refer to weapons and armies in the Hebrew.

Before the temple could be rebuilt, the priestly order had to be right as well as the craftsmen. The spiritual leadership in the priesthood had to be functioning properly, and God corrected both the priestly order in Zechariah 3 and the manual labour in Zechariah 4. He spoke to both realms of authority (spiritual and natural) through the prophetic ministry of Zechariah.

Joshua was a man who was living during that period. (This isn't the same Joshua who trained under Moses and led Israel into the land of promise.) It fell to his lot to be the high priest of Israel at this time. In chapter 3 of the book of Zechariah, the prophet gives a specific word for Joshua, the high priest.

'Then he showed me...'. The prophet is speaking here of the angel who has come and has been dealing with him up to this time. *'...Joshua the high priest...'*. This is a vision in which Zechariah saw a literal man.

With the high priest there were two supernatural personalities present: the angel of the Lord, and Satan. The angel of the Lord as his advocate and Satan at *'...his right hand to oppose him.'* 'Oppose' in this context means 'to accuse, to condemn.' The New American Standard Version reads 'to accuse him.'

Here was Joshua, high priest of Israel, and in Zechariah's vision God showed him what was hindering the temple from being rebuilt. From a spiritual standpoint, the high priest was under the influence of the accuser. The chief reason was that he had allowed his garments to be ruined. Zechariah sees the angel of the Lord standing there and Satan standing at Joshua's right hand to resist and accuse him.

Satan was standing there to resist his work for God. This is why Satan accuses us, that he might resist our efforts in the Kingdom.

The angel of the Lord in the Old Testament was in all likelihood a pre-incarnate appearance of Jesus Christ. I had prepared several pages of reasons why, but have omitted that study until a future time. Many authorities, as you probably know, agree about this point.

> *'Then he showed me Joshua the high priest standing before the Angel of the Lord* [this is Jesus], *and Satan standing at his right hand to oppose* [accuse] *him. And the Lord said to Satan, "The* LORD [Yahweh] *rebuke you, Satan! The* LORD *who has chosen Jerusalem rebuke you! Is this not* [referring to Joshua the high priest] *a brand plucked from the fire?"'*

In other words, 'Isn't Joshua a burning branch that's been snatched out of the fire before being totally consumed?'

Many times the enemy condemns and accuses you with, 'You haven't done this yet. You haven't done that yet. You will never attain to that.' Don't yield to the accuser and be unnecessarily hard on yourself. When Jesus intercedes for you, He refers to you as a 'brand plucked out of the fire.' In other words, a few years ago you were in the fire of judgement and just a step from hell. So what that you are still smouldering a little? You were only recently plucked from the fire. Don't expect too much too soon.

'Now Joshua was clothed with filthy garments, and was standing before the Angel.' (Zechariah 3:3)

The filthy garments that Joshua was clothed with provided the legal grounds for Satan's judicial argument against him. It is as though Satan has been saying, 'God, You shouldn't allow this man to be your high priest. Look at his filthy garments. Look at this problem in his life. Look at that problem in his life.'

Satan condemns and accuses us before God at this very hour, pointing out various things in our lives. Although in our Christian life we have come out of many, many things in which we used to be entangled, we should remember still that our Father is so holy that He cannot look upon evil. He cannot look upon sin (Habakkuk 1:13), and with even so much as an evil thought, without forgiveness and cleansing through Christ, He couldn't accept you with favour in His presence. None of us is able to stand before God alone. However, we can approach Him under the covering of the precious blood of His Son, Jesus.

Joshua was clothed with filthy garments. Joshua wasn't an ungodly man. He was like the rest of us, still falling short of the glory of God. And Satan was using this as his legal ground. Most of what he said about Job was false. Most of what he said about Joshua was true. Yet, God vindicated both of these servants.

When 'the angel of the Lord' rebuked Satan, that was the end of him in the vision. There wasn't a continual battle. One word from 'the angel of the LORD,' and Satan disappears from the passage.

In verse 4 we read,

> *'Then He answered and spoke to those who stood before him* [there may have been other angels standing there], *saying, "Take away the filthy garments from him." '*

As Jesus, our Advocate, intercedes for us asking the Father to have mercy upon us for our sins and failures, the Father accepts His intercessory ministry on our behalf and gives us undeserved kindness. However, our Advocate doesn't stop with a legal pardon. He goes on to change us.

The angel said, 'Take away the filthy garments from him.' Jesus said the same thing to Mary and Martha after Lazarus had come out of the tomb by His power. 'Loose him from his grave clothes and let him go.' Now He is saying to the angels that are in the presence of Joshua, 'Take away the filthy garments from him.' This is sanctification – being made into the image and likeness of God.

A beautiful picture is painted in Zechariah 3 of something wonderful in the believer's life. *'See, I have removed your iniquity from you, and I will clothe you with rich robes'* (Zechariah 3:4), or 'I'll make your present life different.' That's what Jesus says to you today.

There is a difference between our **moral standing** and our **moral state**. Our **moral standing** before God is holy in Christ. Our **moral state** may not be quite so good as our moral standing – to put it mildly!

What God does in the act of justification is to make our standing completely righteous. The perfect righteousness of Christ is credited to our account.

Our state, however, is less than perfect. God wants us to be separate from this present evil age. He wants to bring our 'state' into perfection. He wants the disciple to be like his Master. The Father wants us to go on to perfection. He wants us to lay aside every evil thing and anything that hinders us in our earthly course of perfection – in other words becoming fully mature and reaching completeness in Christ.

In verse 2 Jesus – the special 'angel' – is rebuking Satan on the basis of His righteousness (not Joshua's), and now in verse 4 Jesus is actually effecting a change in Joshua's life. *'See, I have removed your iniquity from you, and I will clothe you with rich robes.'* Only the Son of God has the authority to say that!

In verse 5, Zechariah speaks out in this vision. *'And I said, "Let them put a clean turban on his head."'* In Exodus 28:36–38, a turban such as this is described and has a gold plate in front of it, very much resembling a crown. In fact, sometimes 'turban' is taken to mean crown. This gold plate had engraved on it: *'Holiness to the Lord.'* Zechariah was saying, 'Don't only clothe him with new garments. Also place a crown on his head.' The authority of priesthood is represented in the crown – God's authority, invested in His high priest.

'So they put a clean turban on his head' (Zechariah 3:5), and he took on the appearance of a king with this turban. The priestly garments first; the priestly crown second.

The crown is set upon his head to picture kingly authority. The high priest's ephod pictured Joshua's serving capacity. In Revelation 1:5–6 we read:

> *'To him who loved us, and washed us from our sins in His own blood, and has made us kings and priests to His God and Father . . .'*

Kings to exercise authority, and priests to offer sacrifices.

'And the angel of the Lord stood by' (Zechariah 3:5). He was approving the act by His very presence in front of Joshua as the change of clothes and the clean turban were placed on him. The angel of the Lord was so much as saying, 'I am approving this. I am condoning this.'

'Then the angel of the Lord admonished Joshua . . .', that is, after He cleansed and anointed him, He counselled Joshua.

Now Joshua is clean; he has a fair crown on his head; his garments are white. Now he is given a charge, a responsibility:

> *'Thus says the LORD of hosts: "If you will walk in My ways, and if you will keep My command, then you shall also judge My house . . ."'*   (Zechariah 3:7)

The judges of the book of Judges brought a series of deliverancies to Israel. Samson judged Israel for forty years; Samuel judged Israel for forty years; Deborah judged Israel; that is, they **delivered** Israel. Israel would fall into bondage but later repent and then have to be **delivered** from their enemies.

'Judge My house', God says. God's house needed to be delivered, the temple needed to be cleansed. Jesus wants to cleanse the temple as much in our day as when He entered the outer court of the temple while on earth. That is a mere shadow of what He wants to do now. He wants to enter into the temple, drive out the moneychangers and all the thieves and robbers. He wants to deliver His house, but He is going to do it through people who will walk in His ways and keep His charge.

'If you will walk in My ways' – it is personal obedience to God.

'If you will keep My command' – it is fulfilling your responsibility in the temple as a priest before you are able to judge and deliver His house.

'And likewise have charge of My courts' – it is being entrusted with an expansion of authority from the inner court to the outer court.

'I will give you places to walk among these who stand here' – refers to those in this heavenly vision – 'I'll give you a place here in the temple of God,' the Lord says. This speaks of Joshua's eternal inheritance in the heavenly temple. Jesus promised:

> *'He who overcomes, I will make him a pillar in the temple of My God.'*   (Revelation 3:12)

Jesus, our intercessor

When studying Jesus and His high priestly intercession for us as given in Hebrews chapter 7, I was amazed to find no scripture that implied that Jesus was now praying for the world. One scripture said He did *'make intercession for the transgressors.'* Isaiah chapter 53 speaks of this but was referring to Christ on the cross where He said, *'Father, forgive them, for they do not know what they do'* (Luke 23:34).

All of the Scriptures show Jesus praying for 'them,' referring to believers, as portrayed in these Scriptures:

*' . . . to make intercession for **them**.'*   (Hebrews 7:25)

*' . . . who also makes intercession for **us**.'*   (Romans 8:34)

*'I pray not for the world but for **those whom You have given Me**.'*   (John 17:9)

I wondered why Jesus was not praying for the world. After all, the church is in better shape than the world. But the Lord impressed upon me: 'I'm just going to pray for you. When you are where you ought to be, you are going to take care of the world. I pray for the church. When it gets where it should be, the reaching of the world will be a simple thing.'

The reaching of the world for Christ is simple. But it is the perfecting of the Church that is so hard. Jesus said no man would know the hour of His return, not even the angels, not even the Son, but only the Father. The reason for this is that the Church will have a great part in bringing back the King.

'And this gospel of the kingdom will be preached in all the world as a witness to all the nations, and then the end will come.'   (Matthew 24:14)

We haven't done our job yet. That is why Jesus is praying for us: 'Wake them up Father!'

The whole of Hebrews 7 is a study of Jesus, who, belonging to the order Melchizedek, is our high priest and is continuing to pray for us. He has an unchangeable priesthood in heaven at the Father's right hand. Jesus has been busier since He rose from the dead than He was when He ministered here on earth. While on earth He slept many nights, sometimes He prayed all night; but in heaven, as far as we know, He has prayed continuously for nearly 2,000 years. And we think we have done something when we pray an hour or two!

> *'Therefore He is also able to save to the uttermost those who come to God through Him, since He always lives to **make intercession** for them.'*　　　　　(Hebrews 7:25)

He makes intercession for us and that is why we are saved to the uttermost.

The word 'intercede' means more than just to pray for someone. It means, 'to stand in the place of another.'

We sometimes pray in proxy for people. We understand that it means to 'stand in' for someone, to 'take their place' – 'to intercede.' Jesus, who has a perfect standing, and who is occupying the highest position God ever gave anyone, is standing in your place before the Father for **your** failures, **your** weaknesses, and **your** sins. There is nothing you can do, or cannot do, to affect this advocacy on your behalf.

Actually, we have two advocates – two intercessors. Firstly, Jesus is my advocate. 1 John 2:1–2 tells us,

> *'My little children, these things I write to you, so that you may not sin. And if anyone sins, we have an Advocate with the Father, Jesus Christ the righteous. And He Himself is the propitiation for our sins . . . '*

Jesus said in John 14:16,

> *'And I will pray the Father, and He will give you another Helper.'*

('Helper' could read: intercessor, comforter, strengthener, advocate, counsellor, another to stand by – the Holy Spirit is all these things and more!)

'Another' (the Greek word *allos*) means 'another just like Jesus.' Jesus is my advocate. The same comforter, just like Jesus. Jesus says 'I'll pray and ask the Father to give you another Helper, just like Me – the Holy Spirit.'

To fill the role of an intercessor, one must be possessed by the Spirit of Christ.

At times I've asked people to remember me in prayer. Later, I'd ask them if they prayed for me, and they'd answer, 'Well, yes,' or 'We whispered your name.' Paul begged the Roman Christians to ' ... *strive together with me in prayers to God for me ...* ' (Romans 15:30). This speaks of warfare and rarely do believers war in the Spirit for each other. We make Jesus do all the work!

Some anointed preacher might help you, praying on your behalf, but there is Someone greater who has you on His prayer list. And He calls to the Father on your behalf night and day; and whenever Satan accuses you, He tells him to be silent and He pleads your case. He prays for the needs in your life.

Secondly, the Holy Spirit is your **advocate**. He ministers in those areas of your life where there is a hindrance to God's work taking place. This is the Holy Spirit's ministry. But He cannot intercede for me unless I yield to Him and let Him do it (see Romans 8:26). The only exception would be if He chooses to use another believer to intercede for me by revelation through the Spirit.

Christ intercedes for His church with or without our co-operation. The Holy Spirit can intercede for us **only** as we co-operate.

Satan accused Simon Peter and demanded to have him

Jesus is interceding for us right now, and He gave us an example of what He was going to do before He left the earth. Luke 22:31–32 tells us:

'And the Lord said, "Simon, Simon! Indeed, Satan has asked for you, that he may sift you as wheat. But I have prayed for you..."'

I'm sure Satan has desired to have us also. How does this manifest itself? When he goes to God and says, 'Look at this, look at that. You shouldn't have anything to do with David Alsobrook. Look at how he sometimes becomes angry with his wife. Look at his wavering. Look at how he doubts You and doesn't hold on to Your Word. Hear how he judges others. See how he worries.' These are all terrible things in the sight of God. But Jesus has prayed for me.

No matter what you are going through, know that Jesus is praying on your behalf. 'I have prayed for **you**.' He prayed for Peter before the battle! Do you know that Jesus always gets His prayers answered!

When Satan came and inspected Jesus, he found nothing but purity:

'... the ruler of this world is coming, and he has nothing in Me.' (John 14:30)

Jesus wasn't the only one inspected that night. All the disciples were. Judas certainly was. In Peter especially, Satan found his target. Peter, more than any of the other disciples, was a target, for the keys of the Kingdom had been given to him (Matthew 16:19). He used those keys to open the door of Salvation for the Jews on the day of Pentecost. Ten years later he used those keys to open the door of salvation for the Gentiles through the house of Cornelius. Satan had his sights trained on Peter. That's why you see Peter stumble so badly – he was in a place of high favour. He was the only disciple who ever walked on water, the only disciple who had the keys to the Kingdom given to him. And he was always a third part of that special inner circle: Peter, James and John. He had a special place in the Kingdom of God. Likewise, Satan had a special aim for him.

It was unusual for Jesus to call Peter, 'Simon' (Luke 22:31), because since renaming him, Jesus usually called this Galilean fisherman **Peter**. Peter means '**rock**'. Jesus named him the **rock**. Simon, however, means '**reed**'. Jesus found this reed who was so easily bent by the blowing winds of temptation, overcome by so many fleshly habits, given to a sailor's tongue, and He said, 'I'm going to make you a **rock**.'

True enough, this man, Simon, had acted like a reed sometimes, but like a rock many times too. Because he has this special place, he is an example for Christians. When you read his epistle, he sometimes refers to himself as 'Simon Peter.' The reason is, he learned a great lesson. He learned that he was a reed (Simon) **and** a rock (Peter).

We have much teaching on 'the rock' – in other words, what each of us becomes when we are re-born by the Spirit of God. All of us are part reed and part rock. Before Jesus came along, we were **all** reed. In our flesh dwells no good thing. We are just all flesh. When Jesus came into our life, the truth of 2 Corinthians 5:17 came into effect, and all our old things passed away. Jesus came into our spirits and we became an heir of God and joint heir with Christ (Romans 8:17). We now have all power over the enemy (Luke 10:19), and we are a new creation.

Peter forgot that he was still Simon. When talking to Jesus he sounded like the rock: 'I'm ready to go with you both into prison and to death.' Other 'rock' speeches may sound like: 'Lord, I'm just going to believe for my healing, even if I can't see well without glasses.' 'Lord, I'm not going to eat another bite of food for forty days.' 'Lord, I'll never rebel against You again in any way.' The rock nature really means these promises, but the reed nature will pull us down if we don't properly deal with it.

We have viewed Peter's speech, 'Lord, I'm ready to go with you both into prison and to death' as being solely the boast of pride. Actually, there was a great element of love. This was his realisation of God's ability. This was why he was able to walk on the water with Jesus – he knew Jesus' ability. He'd seen the glory of Jesus with Moses and Elijah on the mountain. He knew the power of Jesus to deliver the demonised boy in the valley.

In John 13:37–38, Jesus is talking to Peter and tells him, 'You are going to deny Me three times.' 'But, I will lay down my life for Your sake!' is Peter's reply. 'You are going to deny Me,' Jesus tells him again. In the English versions chapter 13 ends here. But it is highly possible that the division here is in the wrong place and that the rest of the passage including John 14:4 is spoken to Peter specifically. In that case, Jesus goes on to say to Peter: *'Let not your heart be troubled; you believe in God, believe also in me ... I go to prepare a place for you.'* It was Peter's heart that was troubled:

'What do you mean I'm going to deny You?'

'It's all right son, I'm going to take care of it. You'll make a mess out of it, but I've already prayed for you and soon I'm going to receive you to Myself.' Jesus comforted Peter. Still, it is interesting that in all references to Peter's denial, Jesus forewarned him with the name of 'Simon.'

'Simon, Simon – reed, reed.' And Peter remembers three years before.

'What are You calling me? Call me Peter. Don't You remember what You named me? I am more than a conqueror. My name is Peter – rock.'

Paul was a rock too, but he still realized he had that his old nature to contend with, for in Romans 7:18 he said, *'For I know that in me (that is, in my flesh,) nothing good dwells.'* The secret lies in bringing the flesh into the subjection of the Spirit. That is the secret of Jesus' victory over the enemy!

Peter also needed to bring his flesh into subjection; he was sleeping when he should have been praying. Often I hear 'rocks' say, 'Who needs to pray? I've got faith!'

'Simon, Simon! Indeed, Satan [the adversary] *has asked* [in the Greek the emphasis is 'demanded'] *for you ... '* (Luke

22:31). Evidently, Jesus meant that Satan had gone to God and accused Peter before Him. Evidently the Father alerted Jesus about this through the Holy Spirit, and Jesus then interceded on Simon's behalf before the event ever occurred. *'But I have prayed for you...'* Not, 'I will,' but '**I have**'. *'...that he may sift you as wheat'* (Luke 22:31). 'Simon, he found chaff in you. That reed nature is still there, and he desired to have you.' *'But **I have prayed for you**, that your faith should not fail; and when you have returned to me, strengthen your brethren'* (Luke 22:32).

Jesus knows about all the times when you are going to stumble, just as He knew ahead of time that Peter would fall.

When the Lord saved you, He already knew of every time when you'd deny Him. He knew of every time when you would yield to the tempter. He knew, and prayed for you before these things occurred. He saw other things that would sting and bruise you, but because He continues to uphold you before the Father, interceding on your behalf, you are changed into His image.

The Lord knows of every time that you are going to fail Him. You may say, 'That's it. It is over. Period.' But with the Lord, it is only a comma. Jesus knew that Peter would deny Him, but it was only going to be a 'comma' and not a 'period' in Peter's relationship with the Lord. Hallelujah! That is why Jesus is continually interceding for us.

The blood of sprinkling

> *'But you have come to Mount Zion and to the city of the living God, the heavenly Jerusalem ... to Jesus the Mediator of the new covenant, and to the blood of sprinkling, that speaks better things than that of Abel.'*
>
> (Hebrews 12:22–24)

The New International Version reads, *'the blood of sprinkling, that speaks a better word than Abel's blood spoke.'*

The 'blood of sprinkling' is important. The blood of the atonement lamb which was offered once a year (Yom Kippur) in the nation of Israel (Leviticus 16), was sprinkled on the mercy seat in the holy of holies where the high priest went on the Day of Atonement. Jesus, as our high priest in heaven, shed His blood once at Calvary.

'The blood of sprinkling' refers to the blood on the mercy seat. Chapters 9 and 10 of Hebrews clearly describe how the high priest under the law went into the man-made tabernacle, but Jesus entered into the heavenly temple, not with the blood of bulls and goats, but with His own blood to appear in the presence of God **for us**.

Jesus is now appearing in the presence of God **for us**, on our behalf, as our advocate, a real representative and attorney.

'*...the blood of sprinkling, that speaks a better word than Abel's blood spoke.*' Shed blood speaks! In Genesis 4:10, when God said to Cain, '*The voice of your brother's blood cries out Me from the ground,*' He wasn't speaking figuratively. God can hear the sound of shed blood; it cries out to Him. Abel's blood cried out: 'Vengeance! Vengeance! Judgement!' And so God placed judgement on Cain, a mark of banishment and exile. He was sent away to the land of Nod for the murder of his brother.[1]

Now the 'blood of sprinkling' which is the blood of Jesus on the mercy seat in heaven, speaks 'better things than that of Abel.' It speaks a better word than the blood of Abel spoke. It doesn't cry out for vengeance; it cries out for **mercy**. We overcome the devil by the blood of the Lamb and the word of our vocal agreement here on earth; and when the devil accuses us to God in heaven, Jesus overcomes the devil by His blood on the mercy seat. It is His testimony concerning the blood and our acceptance of it that overcomes the devil.

Satan may say, 'Look at Your servant; look at these areas in his life.' If some of it is true, God cannot say, 'That's absolutely wrong.' Satan appeals to the legal holiness of

God that demands judgement for sin. Then, in the heavenly courtroom, the Judge (God) turns to the Attorney (Jesus) after the Prosecutor (the devil) has made his case and asks, 'What do You have to say?'

'I shed My blood for David, and David accepts My blood,' answers the Attorney.

'Is that all you have to say?'

'Yes, that is all I have to say.'

'Case dismissed,' declares the Judge.

In the Old Testament, in the holy of holies, the Ark of the Covenant had the mercy seat on top of it, and in between were the cherubim. God said that He dwelt 'over the mercy seat.'

So in front of God the father is the blood of Jesus. 1 Peter 1:18–19 tells us,

> '... knowing that you were not redeemed with corruptible things ... but with the precious blood of Christ...'

Now if I was not redeemed with corruptible things, and I was redeemed by the blood, then what is that blood? Incorruptible! Not capable of death! That blood on the mercy seat is just as living as that which flowed in Jesus' veins. It talks. It says, 'Mercy! Mercy!' It speaks a better word. Satan is muzzled before the Father. He is left without a word to say.

The Father of Mercy and God of all Comfort is His legal role of Justice. I'm reminded of a great hymn written by Charles Wesley:

> The Father hears Him pray,
> > His dear Anointed One;
> He cannot turn away
> > the presence of His Son.
> His Spirit answers to the Blood,
> > His Spirit answers to the Blood.
> And tells me I am born of God.

Five bleeding wounds He bears,
    Received on Calvary.
They pour effectual prayers;
    They strongly plead for me.
'Forgive him, Oh forgive,' they cry.
    'Forgive him, Oh forgive,' they cry.
'Let not that ransomed sinner die.'

'Who is he that condemns?' (Romans 8:34) asks. Christ intercedes for us at the Father's right hand. He makes intercession for us. He stands in our place. The Father looks at us in Him, and Jesus says, 'I shed My blood and He accepts My blood.' As long as we are under that blood covering, then we have a continual, perfect, and wonderful salvation. Jesus intercedes for us on the basis of the blood.

Jesus overcomes the accuser in heaven by the blood of the Lamb and the word of His (Jesus') testimony. For us Jesus overcomes the accuser in heaven. Every time Satan accuses us before the Father, Jesus is our legal advocate and technical representative before the Father's right hand. He pleads the merits of His blood. The Father continues His acceptance of us even with all our faults and failures, our sins and shortcomings, because of the perfect righteousness of Jesus and because we truly desire to be pleasing to Him. Every hour that Satan accuses the saints before God, he is cast down by Jesus at the Father's right hand.

In summary of this chapter, I'd like to remind you that the enemy's three primary roles of attack against you are:

1. the tempter;
2. the deceiver;
3. the accuser.

Announce the following decree of liberation to your soul:

'Through the blood of the Lamb and the word of my testimony I can overcome the tempter, the deceiver, and the accuser.'

Say with determination in your heart:

'I'm not going to let **the tempter** overcome me.
'I'm not going to let **the deceiver** overcome me.
'I'm not going to let **the accuser** overcome me.'

Footnote

[1] For a more detailed study on Cain and Abel see chapter 3, entitled 'Why God Accepted Abel's Offering,' of *Understanding the Blood of Christ*. (Sovereign World).

Chapter 3

Overcoming Satan
When He Accuses Others to Me

Now let's study how to overcome the accuser when he accuses fellow Christians to you and me. Note the wording of this Scripture in Revelation 12:10–11:

> 'Then I heard a loud voice saying in heaven, "Now salvation, and strength, and the kingdom of our God, and the power of His Christ have come, for the accuser of our brethren, who accused them before our God day and night, has been cast down. And they overcame him by the blood of the lamb and by the word of their testimony, and they did not love their lives to the death." '

Many Christians become ineffective when Satan comes against them in the role of the accuser of the brethren. In this function he accuses one believer to another. When he accuses us before God, Jesus overcomes that for us every time, perfectly. If only we would overcome Satan to the same degree when he accuses others to us. We must learn to recognise Satan's activities when he accuses the brethren to us, and we must learn how to overcome him when he uses our mouth as a tool to accuse others.

Much of the schism and discord in the Church today is

due to Satan accusing one Christian to another. At times we unwittingly become his tool and voice his very words. The greatest hindrance to unity in the Church today is not diversity of doctrine, affiliation or differences of creed, but discord among the Christians. Satan fights unity in the Church. When the Church becomes unified and stands in its full stature like a mature man, then all men will know that we are Jesus' disciples by the **love** we have one for another.

How subtly the accuser works to fill our minds with accusations about others. Often we think these are our own thoughts, or we may take the accuser's suggestions about our brothers as insights from God and mistakenly call this process the 'gift of discernment.' (There is no general gift of 'discernment.' However, there is a specific gift of 'discerning of spirits.')

We remember that the word *diabolos* from which we get the word 'devil', means 'one who prosecutes as in a court-room.' Another meaning is 'slanderer'. Satan primarily means 'adversary' but secondarily also means 'accuser'. This describes his very nature. To accuse is Satan's highest role of attack against the Church. He is so subtle we often don't even realise he is attacking us.

> 'Now the works of the flesh are evident, which are: ... contentions, jealousies, outbursts of wrath, selfish ambitions, dissensions ... '   (Galatians 5:19–20)

'Dissensions' means 'divisions or factions.' The 'works of the flesh' can only come about in the Church through the believer. Many times in ignorance we yield to the accuser, permitting him to use us as a tool to accomplish 'dissensions'.

The spirit of condemnation has such an inroad into the body of Christ. One reason for this is that the voice of the accuser often comes from the pulpit. God's people have been served heavy yokes and bondages.

The apostle Paul said in Galatians 5:15,

> *'But if you bite and devour one another, beware lest you be consumed by one another!'*

All of the biting and devouring going on in the body of Christ is consuming it from within. The preachers are the most guilty. In some fellowships there is actually little fellowship but much backbiting and devouring. One brother comes against another or slanders the name of a more popular minister.

Mark 7:20–23 tells us in the words of Jesus,

> *'What comes out of the man, that defiles the man. For from within, out of the heart of men, proceed evil thoughts, adulteries, fornications, murders, thefts, covetousness, wickedness, deceit, lewdness, an evil eye, blasphemy, pride, foolishness. All these evil things come from within and defile a man.'*

What is an **evil eye**? It is looking at a person and immediately thinking evil. We look at them to discover what is wrong with them. We desire to see what wrong they reflect.

An evil eye is in operation when a person who has no merit for his judgement looks upon someone and instantly judges them from the outward appearance. In 2 Corinthians 5:12 Paul talked about, '. . . *those who boast in appearance and not in heart.'* This is what the Bible calls an 'evil eye'. It is looking on someone with suspicion. The accused have done nothing and said nothing. Nothing firsthand is known about the person. This is an evil eye. This defiles not only the individual that has the evil eye, but often the whole body. Suspicion is very contagious.

In one church, a person said to me, 'I have the gift of discernment. I discern a very bad spirit about you.' After a while I realised that this person didn't have a revelation from the Lord, just a plain old suspicion. An evil eye is a spiritual operation, but one that does not come from the Holy Spirit. Its source is the accuser of the brethren.

In Proverbs 6:16–18 Solomon said,

> *'These six things the LORD hates, yes seven are an abomination to Him.'*

He is saying that God hates six specific sins, but the seventh is in a class all by itself. Of course the Lord hates all seven things, but the seventh in the list is a special abomination before God. In that list He talks about pride, murder, lying, wickedness ... but the seventh thing, the greatest abomination to God is *'... one who sows discord among brethren.'* It is hard to believe that God hates discord sowing in the Church more than he despises murder in the world, yet a man full of wisdom said such is the case.

Judge with righteous judgement

The apostle Paul reproved those who gloried in appearance and not in heart:

> *'... that you may have an answer for those who boast in appearance and not in heart ... Therefore, from now on, we regard no one according to the flesh ... '*
>
> (2 Corinthians 5:12, 16)

We are not to judge a man, a minister or a fellow Christian, according to the flesh – in other words by the outward order of things. Often we evaluate a ministry's effectiveness by its outward growth, or by its numerical size, or by monetary growth, or by some other facet of natural things – the car the minister drives, the kind of clothes he wears etc. We tend to judge success from a natural standpoint. Just because a ministry has flourished does not mean it is necessarily of God.

Success does not necessarily denote godliness, although commercial success is one of the end-time signs in the Church. Paul said to Timothy that financial success during the latter times would become very popular and that godliness would be a means to gain (1 Timothy 6:5). The more wealth a minister amasses today, the more godly he is considered to be. We should not judge the effectiveness of someone's ministry by these standards! We should learn how to **judge with righteous judgement**.

Recently I heard a brother say, 'Satan isn't fighting unity.' 'What do you mean?' I asked. He replied, 'Satan has the Christians doing it for him.'

Truly, it is Satan behind Christians who are devouring one another. We need to look to the Word and let the Word show us where we have allowed the accuser of the brethren to use us to aid his work.

John 7:24 states,

> *'Do not judge according to appearance, but judge with righteous judgement.'*

If you judge by appearance it is the god of this world who could be influencing your judgement. **Judge with righteous judgement**. Know no man according to the flesh. Don't judge a minister or brother by the flesh.

A lady I know once told me about an extremely obese preacher and what a great blessing she received from his ministry. I said to her, 'You know there is bound to be something wrong because of his outward appearance.' I'll never forget what she said: 'Yes, but I've learned not to evaluate that man's spirit by his outward appearance. I know that in his personal life there must be something that is not as it should be, but I've learned not to judge by appearance. I've learned to receive in the Spirit what God has for me in his ministry.' She was judging with righteous judgement. How slow we are to perceive spiritual things but not so with Jesus.

Usually when someone asks me to discern something in the Spirit it takes me a while to get the understanding. I told a prophet that I was having sinus problems. Immediately he replied, 'This came on you when you were twelve,' and proceeded to tell me other things. He had no way of knowing that when I was in the sixth grade I had a sinus attack, was hospitalised and missed twenty-nine days of one semester of school. This brother had such a 'quick understanding in the fear of the Lord,' it didn't take him long to receive revelation about my condition.

My flow of revelation is not that quick, and I need to learn not to judge with my eyes. The Lord is having to teach me along this line.

We can easily find ourselves saying, 'Yes, this brother is given to this or that. He sure is shallow.' All the time we think we are dealing in a spiritual realm, when actually we are dealing in the flesh. If we are going to become perfect and mature, we are going to have to be blind to the natural appearance. We are not to judge by the outward appearance – we are to judge with righteous judgement.

'What do you think about this man's ministry?' I'm frequently asked. If I reply, 'Well, I have heard one thing about him,' then I could easily cast him in a derogatory light. Even though I don't realise it, I may have put him in a negative category.

One thing I've learned is that every preacher has an off night. I used to say, 'I'll go and hear anyone speak once.' Now I say, 'I'll go and hear anyone speak two or three times before I form an opinion.'

Several years ago I went to hear a well-known evangelist. To me, at the time, I felt that pride and arrogance were pouring forth from him. I went away praying, 'Oh, God, how can You be in that? I can't see You at all in this and I can't see why others see so much in him.' My peace was gone; and between the Lord and me, my prayer life wasn't flowing. For several days afterwards every time I praised the Lord, it was empty and hollow sounding. The Lord reminded me, 'Blessed are the pure in heart for they shall see God.' I repented and got my heart right towards this minister and went to another meeting. God was able to allow me to properly evaluate the man and his ministry. I got my heart pure towards God and was able to overlook the outward things, leaving them for God to deal with; and did I see God! I was thrilled and saw God do some great works. I learned something important about preachers: there is not one who is all wheat. We are all a mixture. There is nothing in our ministries today that is all good or all evil. (There are false prophets, of course, but I am speaking of those who are serving the Lord.) We are to prove all things, to hold fast that part which is good, and to abstain from all appearance of evil – all the chaff.

A Christian once came to me saying, 'I just love your tapes. I've heard thirty or forty. But on this one I disagreed so much I've not been able to listen to any more of your tapes.' It was such a minor thing he disagreed with that I was surprised at his strong reaction.

I replied, 'You need to realise I'm just a man like yourself. My teaching has some parts of God and some parts of me; and you'll just have to learn how to weigh, to evaluate, and to judge with righteous judgement. But don't let the accuser throw me out just because of one little thing.'

Ephesians 4:32 tells us: *'Be kind to one another.'* The word 'kind' is the same word used in Matthew 11:30 when Jesus said, 'My yoke is easy'. It should be easy to be yoked one to another.

I have heard some people say, 'That particular minister has nothing to say.' And I go to hear him with a preconceived notion and judgement that I have not arrived at by actually receiving his ministry. I've learned that sometimes that very same person I've heard so much bad about will minister to me in such a beautiful way. I'm learning slowly, but surely, to judge with righteous judgement.

Let's check in John's Gospel where Jesus judged with righteous judgement:

> *'Now when He was in Jerusalem at the Passover, during the feast, many believed in His name, when they saw the signs which He did. But Jesus did not commit Himself to them, because He knew all men, and had no need that anyone should testify of man, for He knew what was in man.'*
>
> (John 2:23–25)

Every time you say, 'What about so and so? What about him? What did you feel about her?' think of this verse. Jesus was not this way. He *'had no need that anyone should testify of man.'* He didn't need anyone to tell Him what another person was like. You would never hear Jesus ask any questions such as: 'Peter, have you noticed anything strange about John lately? I was just wondering.' Jesus didn't need anyone to give evidence about another person. He already knew what was in a person.

> *'For the eyes of the LORD run to and fro throughout the whole earth, to show Himself strong on behalf of those whose heart is loyal to Him.'*   (2 Chronicles 16:9)

We know that His eyes are always upon the righteous, according to Psalm 34:15, and yet He still has to look over all the earth to find those whose heart is perfect toward Him. God judges heart attitudes, and we need to judge with a righteous judgement.

If a brother or sister stumbles in sin we need to judge with a righteous judgement. When a minister stumbles, immediately you hear all the other ministers talking about him. Be careful what kind of judgement you render, for God is going to let you be judged by the same measure of judgement. When we hear something bad about someone, how quick we are to evaluate, to surmise, and to formulate our opinion about him, even before we take it to God in prayer. We are so quick to judge by what we see with our eyes. God wants us to use righteous judgement and not to be used by the accuser.

I've heard some dreadful things said about ministers. I'd think that they were truly bad and that they had better repent. Then, after some years of travel, I heard through the grapevine that some people were saying I had a Cadillac back home, that I owned two homes, and that I did all kinds of terrible things. I'd never even owned a car, let alone a Cadillac and I didn't own one house, let alone two. I said, 'God, those are dreadful things people are saying. They are lies.' The Lord let me ride along for a while as I was praying about this. Then, suddenly I remembered that someone had gossiped to me, 'Oh, did you hear about brother so and so? He does this, and he does that and the other.' The Lord reminded me how quick I had been to believe that report. I repented.

We grow up learning how to assess and judge in the natural, and it's hard for us to learn how to judge in the spiritual. One example of this truth is found in Acts 9, but let me preface my remarks about the treatment of Saul.

We often think of the New Testament church as being perfect. **It was far from perfection!** In Acts 9 there is an example of Satan accusing a brother to the other Christians and causing suspicion and the rejection of the brother. If it hadn't been for one man – Barnabas – who knew how to judge with a righteous judgement, Saul might have been permanently bruised.

Acts 9 is all about Saul, a hot-headed zealot. Jesus apprehended him on the road to Damascus with a dazzling light.

Jesus appeared to Ananias and told him to '... *go to the street called Straight, and inquire at the house of Judas for one called Saul of Tarsus, for behold, he is praying'* (Acts 9:11). Was he willing to go? No, he immediately began to give God a news report: 'Lord, haven't You heard what terrible things this man has done to Your saints in Jerusalem?' Ananias argued with the Lord. But the Lord said to him, *'Go, for he is a chosen vessel of Mine...'* The Lord isn't given much to explanation, He just says, '**Go**' and then also tells Ananias of the things that Saul must suffer. That day Saul became a vibrant believer.

'And when Saul had come to Jerusalem [the apostles' head-quarters, for the Gospel was first preached where the outpouring at Pentecost had occurred], *he tried to join the disciples; but they were all afraid of him, and did not believe that he was a disciple'* (Acts 9:26). The Scripture doesn't say, 'When **Paul** had come.' It says, 'When **Saul** had come.' He was still unrecognised. It is hard for me to picture Christians who never quoted Paul, but such was the case.

Let us use our imaginations concerning the young convert's attempt to join the disciples:

'But I've repented! I had a dazzling light out on the road.'

'Were any of the brothers with you when that happened?'

'No, I wasn't a Christian then, so I certainly wouldn't be with Christians when that happened.'

'The Scripture says out of the mouth of two or three witnesses shall every word be established.'

'But I really have repented. I'm sorry for all the havoc I wrought, and I have been forgiven for having thrown your relatives in jail.'

Imagine all he had to overcome!

There was no forgiveness or trust toward this new brother. They had relatives and friends who were in jail because of Saul's work against them. We see in them the accusation of Satan. If there was anything Satan did not want, it was for Saul to become a functioning part of the Church. He wanted to do everything he could to keep Saul away. Satan went around whispering in their ears: 'He's not a believer!' 'Don't listen to him.' 'Don't believe him.' 'This is the man who is spying out the Church.' 'He's the ringleader.' 'Be careful, don't get too friendly with him.' Whisper. Whisper. The whisperings of Satan caused the Christians to be afraid of Saul.

Saul didn't get many hugs when he went to Jerusalem. I know how he felt. I imagine he got some hugs like ones I've received! I go to a new place and feel conspicuous. Then here come the elders. Oh, yes, they want to hug you. (I'd rather just stick with the old-fashioned handshake.) Praise God for the elders! In five seconds they expect me to give a rundown of all my background. They give me a scrutinising gaze from the top of my head to the soles of my feet and ask, 'Are you married?' 'Do you have your bills paid back home?' They interrogate me like detectives instead of praying for me before the meeting. I feel like an ox going to the slaughter, or like a lamb before the shearers. Their line of thinking seems to be that no one can or should cast out devils in Jesus' name and not follow them.

Can you picture yourself in Saul's place? *'...they were all afraid of him and did not believe that he was a disciple.'* And don't you know he would have finished it all if he had said, 'I'm going to preach before kings. Thousands of Gentiles will be saved through my preaching.'

But, thank God for Barnabas who overcame the accuser's lies to his ears, by the power of Jesus' blood for that new disciple:

> *'But Barnabas took him and brought him to the apostles. And he declared to them how he had seen the Lord on the road, and that he had spoken to him, and how he had preached boldly at Damascus in the name of Jesus. So he was with them at Jerusalem, coming in and going out.'*
>
> (Acts 9:27–28)

This dear brother knew not to judge by outward appearance. He did not judge according to Saul's past. He knew to judge with righteous judgement.

I was asked to teach in a certain city and a brother there said about me: 'Well, I don't know about him. I don't agree with him on everything. I had a check about him in a certain area at one time.' Another Christian looked at him and commented, 'Well, I've had several checks about you all along!'

It is so easy to look for something negative. We go to meetings and see what we can find wrong with a particular minister. Romans 14:4 asks,

> *'Who are you to judge another's servant? To his own master he stands or falls. Indeed, he will be made to stand, for God is able to make him stand.'*

Concerning Christian brothers and sisters – all of them are another man's servant. They are servants of the Lord Jesus. So who am I to sit in judgement on them? They will stand before the judgement seat of Christ, so who am I to judge the Lord's servant?

In Romans 14:10 the question is asked, 'But why do you judge your brother? Or why do you show contempt for your brother?' How frequently we are guilty of asking others, 'Did you hear that preacher? Is he all right?' Often the answer is, 'Well, I guess he's all right.' This answer sets him at nothing immediately.

A certain well-known minister acts very silly in the pulpit. I wondered about him and once asked another very well-known teacher about him. 'What do you think about him?' I asked. The man looked at me and commented, 'He is God's problem!'

This is quite correct! That man does not have to stand and give an account to you or me. Any pastor, of course, must use wisdom and spiritual discernment in asking guest speakers to fill his pulpit.

> *'Therefore let us not judge one another any more, but rather resolve this, not to put a stumbling block or a cause to fall in our brother's way.'* (Romans 14:13)

There are some people we would rather not sit by in church. We wouldn't say it, but it is true. There are some people we prefer to avoid.

Jesus was free with everyone. He could sit down with the

publican or with the magistrate. He could freely socialize with the greatest to the least.

We have to repent of judging the wrong way, because we have been yielding to the accuser. The only way we are going to overcome is by the blood of Christ and by the word of our testimony. We need to ask for the blood to cleanse us and then to confess the merits of Jesus' blood for our brother and sister. When Satan comes to us with: 'Look at him, look at her,' we should say, 'they accept the blood of Jesus, and they are righteous because of the blood.'

There are some who are weaker in the faith than others, who have obvious spots in their garments. We often turn away from them when we could minister to them and restore them. The Christian army is the only army that kicks its wounded. In earthly wars when a soldier's fellow comrade is shot down, he will risk life and limb right out on the battlefield to pick up his friend and carry him to safety. But let the brother on the front line of spiritual battle drop his shield one way or the other, allowing a fiery dart to hit him, and often his comrades will run out to him and say, 'Why did you let the devil do that to you?' and give him a sharp kick in his already-hurting side.

Let a man of God fall one way or the other and you'll hear righteous indignation all over the country pounding that man. All the many years he may have served God, all the many trials and secret burdens he may have carried for the cause of Christ are forgotten. That one tragedy is remembered. Long after God has forgiven and forgotten it, people remember. We bite each other like cannibals.

> *'But if you bite and devour one another, beware lest you be consumed by one another!'* (Galatians 5:15)

Don't judge, in case you yourself are judged. Judge with the wrong kind of judgement, and it will come right back to you. In fact, that may be the only reason most of us want to stop judging the wrong way; we don't like being judged the wrong way either!

Test the spirits

People recognised Jesus of Nazareth by His appearance, by His mannerisms, and by His physical traits for a few brief years. We are not able know Him that way any more; we know Him in the Spirit. We don't know Him in the flesh, but by the revelation of the Holy Spirit. That is also how we are to know a fellow Christian.

I was in an area and a pastor came to the meeting. After the meeting we went to eat and fellowship. Soon I found it was going to be a question-and-answer time – it wasn't a time for fellowship at all. It was a time for finding out what kind of doctrine I believed. But 1 John 4:1–4 makes it very clear that we are to try every **spirit**.

> *'Beloved, do not believe every spirit, but **test the spirits**, whether they are of God; because many false prophets have gone out into the world.'*

Test the spirits. Don't judge by the flesh. No guest speaker is stupid enough to say something obviously controversial like, 'I don't believe Jesus was born of a virgin.' A false teacher will have all the right answers at first, slowly introducing heresy as he gains people's confidence. Jesus taught that outwardly a wolf appears to be a sheep. No, **test the spirits** to see whether they are of God. You cannot very well do that unless you are in the right spirit yourself.

> *'Do not judge according to appearance, but judge with righteous judgement.'*　　　　　　　　　　(John 7:24)

If we are to be able to overcome the accuser when he accuses others to us, we must remember those good questions Paul gave us in Romans 14:10:

'But why do you judge your brother? Or why do you show contempt for your brother?'

A good principle to follow in this regard is: *'... let us not judge one another anymore ... '* (verse 13). 'Judge' in this sense means 'to condemn.' Rather we are only to judge in the sense of evaluation, weighing those who labour among us. Paul said, *'He who is spiritual judges all things'* (1 Corinthians 2:15). In a spiritual sense we are to weigh, but we are not to condemn.

If you have been guilty of judging, of letting the accuser of the brethren use you by whispering in your ear, overcome him by the blood of Jesus. Don't look for the bad in your brother or sister; look for the good.

When people come to me with a negative attitude – especially if I'm not walking in the Spirit – I will tend to react negatively. But when people come with a positive attitude, 'Brother, I believe Jesus Christ is in you' (2 Corinthians 13:5), or 'I came to see Jesus,' they draw something good right out of me. It is so beautiful when people can get a word from the Lord.

I've been in meetings when whole crowds have been swayed by the accuser of the brethren because of negative binding attitudes. Some have come looking only for the bad.

There will always be something about a person with which we don't agree, or that we are not in harmony with. So, instead of looking at that with which we don't agree, we must start looking for Jesus Christ in that person. We need to bring a good report about them and say, 'Jesus Christ is in you, the hope of glory. I know that you have areas in your life the Lord is working on and ironing out, but I'm believing to see Jesus Christ in you.'

We are too quick to judge, saying, 'Shape up or ship out.' Let us not judge one another any more. Let's judge with righteous judgement.

Believers are not to be in wrangling arguments. *'... let us walk by the same rule, let us be of the same mind'* (Philippians

3:16). 'Let us be in harmony with one another' Paul is saying. Learn not to yield to the accuser of the brethren when he accuses others to us.

Subtle voices also come to us; we have to learn how to deal with the accuser of the brethren who is a whisperer of lies. Let me give you an example:

I'm driving down the highway. Suddenly the thought comes to me: 'You know, Brother so and so wasn't very responsive to you the last time you were there.' (Maybe he didn't go out of his way to show kindness to you.) 'You really ought to be careful about that man.' Satan whispered that in my ear.

If I don't discern that that voice is coming from Satan and reject it, what is going to happen? Satan is going to go to that brother miles away and say: 'You know, David Alsobrook really didn't have quite enough love toward you, did he?' When we come together the next time, a wall will exist between us. There will be a reserve. My brother-in-law, Jim Maloney, refers to these inward reservations as 'heart measles.'

There isn't a single preacher who has not had the accuser of the brethren work overtime on his behalf around other ministers, around other Christians, around other fellowships, and has not known what it is to go around with every eye on him.

'Therefore let us not judge one another any more.' This doesn't mean that we are not to evaluate others properly in the Spirit. But the sense of the word in Romans 14:30 is that of condemning our brothers and sisters in Christ. We are to 'judge' each other only in the sense that we ascertain a need and minister to it (see Galatians 6:1–2).

Don't judge by appearances

Two passages in Isaiah speak of how Jesus would judge and how He would not judge. To follow the example Jesus set forth is always a wise principle.

Isaiah 42:19 records some strange words about the Servant that the Lord says He will send:

> *'Who is blind but My servant, or deaf as My messenger whom I send? Who is blind as he that is perfect, and blind as the LORD'S servant?'*

Doesn't it seem strange that Lord's servant is to be blind? The Lord's messenger is to be deaf? Think of it: the messenger that God is going to send will be blind and deaf!

In the preceding verse though, we read: *'Hear, you deaf; and look, you blind, that you may see'* (Isaiah 42:18). That is exactly what happened when Jesus came. The deaf heard and the blind saw. Yet the Word says of Him that although He will open the ears of the deaf and the eyes of the blind, He is both blind and deaf. We know that this cannot be a blindness and a deafness concerning His physical eyes and ears, for verse 20 reads:

> *'Seeing many things, but you do not observe* [in other words seeing many things but paying little regard to them]; *opening the ears, but he does not hear.'*

'Who is blind as he that is perfect, and blind as the LORD's servant?' The prophecy stated of Jesus. This paradox is one of those holy riddles we sometimes find in the Word of God.

Let us see how He is blind.

The first few verses of Isaiah chapter 11 deal with the first coming of Jesus, and the last several verses deal with the Second Coming. Verse one is one of the messianic promises of Jesus, the Branch that would grow out of Jesse's root. Verse two reads,

> *'The spirit of the LORD shall rest upon him, the spirit of wisdom and understanding, the spirit of counsel and might, the spirit of knowledge and of the fear of the LORD.'*

Here are seven attributes of God's Spirit. John 3:36 states that Jesus had the Spirit without measure; this means not only in quantity but also in all operations.

1. The Spirit of the LORD (Yahweh – the Father) shall rest upon Him.
2. The spirit of wisdom.
3. The spirit of understanding.
4. The spirit of counsel.
5. The spirit of might.
6. The spirit of knowledge.
7. The spirit of the fear of the LORD.

We read in the Book of Revelation (Revelation 1:4; 3:1; 4:5; 5:6) of the seven spirits of God, or the sevenfold Holy Spirit.

Jesus had the Spirit of the Lord; the Dove rested upon Him so that He could heal the bruised and deliver the oppressed (Luke 4:18). He had the spirit of wisdom and understanding so that He would know how to answer the questions of the scribes and the Pharisees. He used the spirit of counsel and might in His prophetic ministry. Later we'll see how He used the spirit of knowledge and of the fear of the Lord.

Isaiah 11:3,

> *'His delight is in the fear of the LORD, and he shall not judge by the sight of his eyes.'*

In what way would Jesus be blind? *'He shall not judge by the sight of his eyes.'* His physical eyes would be quite able to see, but He wouldn't make decisions based merely on what He saw. How was He deaf? In the same way He wouldn't render a decision based purely on what His ears heard. *'But with righteousness he shall judge.'*

We have already mentioned that John's Gospel told how Jesus judged:

> *'Do not judge according to the appearance, but judge with righteous judgement.'*

'Appearance' means don't judge by what you see with your eyes. Isaiah 11:3–4 fits in so beautifully with John 7:24.

> *'But with righteousness he shall judge* [literally 'deliver'] *the poor.'*

The problem is that the accuser gets us to sit in judgement. We are guilty of this because we walk according to the appearance of things.

Let us take one more example from the Gospel of John which shows how Jesus practised the fulfilment of the prophecies given in Isaiah.

Jesus' methods of judging are portrayed in John chapter 2 and chapter 8. Isaiah clearly taught that the Messiah would not judge by the sight of His eyes or by what He heard with His ears, but with righteousness would He judge. He would have a quick perception, a quick knowing in the fear of the Lord.

John 2:23–24:

> *'Now when He was in Jerusalem at the Passover, during the feast, many believed in His name when they saw the signs which He did. But Jesus did not commit Himself to them, because He knew all men.'*

This is strange indeed. He is at Jerusalem at the Passover on a feast day and has an outstanding meeting. Many people believe in Him when they see the miracles He does. (If He had produced a magazine for His ministry, it would have been the meeting of the month!) According to the natural eye it appears to be an outstanding success. He is so wonderfully received. Many are believing – many seeing tremendous miracles – a great time, yet Jesus shows no elation over the meeting. *'But Jesus did not commit Himself to them.'* It must have seemed strange to His disciples. Jesus was not carried away with all of this '... *because He knew all men, and had no need that anyone should testify of man, for He knew what was in man.'* Jesus did not need anyone to tell Him what another person was like.

The narrative in John 2:25 ends the chapter, but in the original text, no chapter division should occur there. The words following are actually an example of Jesus' knowing what was in man.

> *'There was a man of the Pharisees, named Nicodemus, a ruler of the Jews . . . '*

This man is really somebody. This is a teacher's teacher, a preacher's preacher. This is the elite of the spiritual hobnob of Jerusalem. And yet Jesus said, 'Nicodemus, you need to be born again.' Jesus knew what was in him. How did He know what was in man? Because the knowledge of the Lord was upon Him, the quick understanding in the fear of the Lord. He didn't judge by the sight of His eyes.

Neither did Jesus judge 'by the hearing of His ears.' Possibly some said of Nicodemus, 'He's one of the most spiritual persons in all of Israel.' But Jesus judged with righteousness. He saw the inward spirit of the man, and it was quite dead.

Another example is found in John, chapter 8, that fulfils the Isaiah prophecy:

> *'But Jesus went to the mount of Olives. Now early in the morning He came again into the temple, and all the people came to Him; and He sat down and taught them. The scribes and Pharisees brought to Him a woman caught in adultery. And when they had set her in the midst, they said to Him, "Teacher, this woman was caught in adultery, in the very act. Now Moses, in the law, commanded us that such should be stoned. But what do you say?" This they said, testing Him, that they might have something of which*

> *to accuse Him. But Jesus stooped down and wrote on the*
> *ground with His finger, as though He did not hear.'*
> (John 8:2–6)

He doesn't make any decision by what His ears hear. He sees many things and pays no attention to them – 'As though He did not hear them.' He opens deaf ears and yet doesn't hear with His own ears.

Some theologians purport the idea that this incident was a set-up. According to this view the woman wasn't actually an adulteress, but an actress. The Pharisees were hoping to embarrass Christ by putting Him into a position where He would pass judgement for adultery on an innocent individual. The people would then know He was not a true prophet and His ministry would be permanently discredited. However, if one accepts the Word of God as his standard this woman surely was the adulteress the Pharisees said she was because Jesus exhorted her to *'sin no more'* (verse 11), after all her judges had left the scene.

The truth is, the Pharisees showed their bigotry, hypocrisy, and partiality in that they only brought the woman, and not the man also. *'Teacher, she was caught in adultery, in the very act.'* Well, what did they do with the man? They didn't bring him. Moses taught that both parties were to be stoned. Yet, these scribes and Pharisees brought only the woman.

Notice that Jesus was at the temple (verse 2), and many people were around Him. The people at the temple knew the law of Moses. These people were conditioned only by the law. Jesus couldn't explain the soon-to-come new covenant and the grace of God. In fact, Jesus couldn't even explain grace and the new covenant to His closest disciples. He said in John 16:12,

> *'I still have many things to say to you, but you cannot bear*
> *them now. However, when He, the Spirit of truth, has come,*
> *He will guide you into all truth.'*

Since all men were so firmly entrenched in the belief that one must be circumcised to be saved, it took the Holy Spirit ten years after Pentecost to teach them that a Gentile could be saved without that rite. Jesus, therefore, could not explain to these people the purpose for which He was sent. These people walked by the Word, and the Word then was only the Old Testament; and it said irrevocably that an adulterer and adulteress are to be stoned to death without mercy.

Jesus was sent by the Father not to condemn the world, but so that the world through Him might be saved (John 3:17). He was sent not to reveal the law of God, but the grace of God (John 1:17). He was between a rock and a hard place. If He had said, 'Don't stone her,' then those present would have said, 'This man is a false prophet' for He would have been opposing the law of Moses and would have fallen into disrepute with the people. If Jesus had said, 'Stone her,' then He would have been compromising His conviction and thwarting the purpose of His mission; for the Father didn't send Him into the world to condemn it, but to save it. He didn't come to destroy, He came to save those who were lost (Luke 19:10). At one time when the disciples said to Him, 'They won't receive You here, do You want us to command fire to come down?' He answered, 'You don't even know what spirit you are of.'

> ' "Now Moses, in the law, commanded us that such should be stoned. But what do you say?" This they said, testing Him, that they might have something of which to accuse Him. But Jesus stooped down and wrote on the ground with His finger, as though He did not hear.'

I believe He was writing various Scriptures on the ground, about the Lord's mercy and love.

In verse 7 Jesus gave the perfect answer:

> 'So when they continued asking Him, He raised Himself up

> *and said to them, "He who is without sin among you, let*
> *him throw a stone at her first." '* (John 8:7)

That is to say, 'the sinner shall be stoned, but the sinner must be stoned by sinless stone-throwers.'

That even sounded good according to the Law of Moses. Now doesn't that make sense? If you are going to stone a sinner, you, as stone-throwers, should be sinless. In saying this, He doesn't refute the Law of Moses, nor does He compromise His mission. The 'spirit of wisdom and understanding' was upon Him.

The Pharisees were men who were not ready to admit their own sins. Usually they said in effect to Jesus, 'We see, we are not blind. We are of God, You are of the devil,' etc. But here Jesus did something. In verse 7 He said that only the sinless stone-throwers may stone the sinner and then He again stooped down and wrote some more on the ground.

> *'The those who heard it, being convicted by their conscience,*
> *went out one by one, beginning with the oldest even to the*
> *last. And Jesus was left alone, and the woman standing in*
> *the midst.'* (John 8:9)

They went out one by one. Why didn't they all go out together? *'Beginning with the oldest even to the last.'* Beginning with the oldest Pharisee and ending with the youngest Pharisee.

He must have gotten the attention of the oldest Pharisee. Perhaps when He stooped down He wrote in the sand in classical Hebrew, so that no one standing around could read it but the educated Pharisee. Maybe He wrote his chief, most grievous sin, and being convicted by what he had heard and saw – his own greatest failure before God – he was convicted by his own conscience and went out first.

Then Jesus looked at the next in line. He's the next 'super

righteous.' He's the one who, if asked, 'Are you righteous?' would reply, 'Oh, am I righteous? I fast twice a week, I give tithes of everything I own.' Jesus caught his attention and wrote his sin on the ground. Being convicted by what he heard and by what he had read, he went out also. Perhaps Jesus wrote the name of someone that the Pharisee had sinned against. Only that Pharisee understood what the name meant as the strange prophet wrote it in the earth.

Those now leaving were the same men who were dragging the woman through the street a short time before, they who would not relax their grip on her wrists as they hauled her before Jesus. Jesus kept on writing on the ground until they all left. They went out one by one, beginning with the oldest to the youngest. What He wrote, every man knew He had no way of knowing. It was revealed to Him by God. He couldn't condone sin, but the sin within their hearts was as great as the sin of her acts, and if one should be stoned, all should be stoned. Jesus didn't need any man to tell Him what a person was like, for He knew what was in man. He didn't judge according to appearance, He judged with righteous judgement.

Then,

> 'When Jesus had raised Himself up, and saw no one but the woman, He said to her, "Woman, where are those accusers of yours? Has no one condemned you?" She said, "No one, Lord." And Jesus said to her, "Neither do I condemn you; go, and sin no more."' (John 8:10–11)

'Where are those accusers of yours?' We become accusers, instruments of the accuser whenever we judge by outward appearances. We look at the flesh instead of seeking to know by the Spirit. Jesus did not look at a person and judge by the flesh; He knew a person by the Spirit.

In 2 Corinthians 5:16 Paul spoke to the Corinthian church, who were guilty of glorying in appearance and not in heart. They were guilty of thinking they were a super church with super apostles. They were super-duper wonder workers. They gloried in men. Paul said, 'Your glorying is not good.' They might have said, 'Have you been to that preacher's meeting?' 'Have you heard this man?' Then to others who were truly ministers of God, they might have paid little regard. Even of Paul himself they said, 'He writes pretty good letters, but his personal presence is weak. He is unimpressive. He's not even a good speaker.'

In response Paul said,

> *'Therefore, from now on, we regard no one according to the flesh. Even though we have known Christ according to the flesh, yet now we know Him thus no longer.'*
>
> (2 Corinthians 5:16)

That's why there are no original paintings of Christ today. God knew we would want to imitate the flesh; whereas He wants to form Christ within our souls. All the things we know about Jesus today are what we've learned about Him by the Spirit and the Word. Paul taught us that, in the very same way we know Jesus – by the Spirit – we are also to know every person among us.

Am I my brother's keeper?

The attitude many Christians seem to have is: 'Am I my brother's keeper?' This is the Cain spirit and a wrong attitude. It robs us. We are not to look only after ourselves, but we are to look after our brother also. We are to bear one another's burdens and so fulfil the law of Christ. If a brother is not an overcomer, are we to kick him? That is what the accuser wants us to do. If our brother stumbles in some outward sin, we will find many saints who will be ready to kick him.

There is a way to identify a fault in a brother or sister that does not bring a sense of condemnation. In Zechariah 3, the angel of the Lord said to Joshua that if he would keep God's ways, he would deliver His house. Before we can judge, we must be sure we are walking closely to God. He wants us to be able to judge with righteous judgement. He that is spiritual judges all things (1 Corinthians 2:15). We are to judge without a sense of condemnation or retaliation. We are to judge on a one-to-one basis. If our brother sins against us, are we first to call our best friend and tell him all about it? No. We should be the first to go to that person and gently explain what has happened **alone** (see Matthew 18). This is the correct way. This keeps the slanderer from accusing the body of Christ.

God grant that when a brother or sister resists you in a particular truth, you won't let the accuser of the brethren build a wall of defensiveness in you against him or her.

Three things greatly hinder the power of God in the Church. They grieve Christ and quench the moving of His healing power. They are outlined in Isaiah 58:6–9. Israel asked, *'Why have we fasted ... and You have not seen?'* (Isaiah 58:3). God then gives them three reasons why they were not receiving healing power:

1. The yoke of not letting the oppressed go free (legalism);
2. Pointing the finger (criticism, fault-finding); and
3. Speaking vanities (insincerity in speech).

All of these hindrances are the influence of the accuser.

Sadly, we are quick to judge the wrong way, and slow to judge the right way. Matthew 7:1 tells us in these very familiar words: *'Judge not, that you be not judged.'* Sometimes the Word says, 'don't judge,' and sometimes it says 'judge.' This is not a contradiction, but a **contradistinction**. Note Paul's admonition in 1 Corinthians 2:15:

> *'But he who is spiritual judges* [discerns] *all things, yet he himself is rightly judged by no one.'*

That is, he weighs all things, he judges all things. Note also the wording, *'he that is spiritual judges all things'.*

There are shades of meaning in the word 'judge.' One of the most common meanings is 'to deliver.' Believers are to 'judge' or 'deliver' a brother or sister. In Matthew 7:1 the meaning here is not that we are not to sit in judgement, but we are to deliver. The wrong way to judge would be to sit in judgement. There will come a time when we will sit in judgement, we will even judge the angels, but until that time we judge no one (see 1 Corinthians 4:5).

Verse 4 tends to be the only part of the Matthew 7 Scripture that gets quoted, but it continues:

> *'Judge not, that you be not judged. For ... with the measure you use, it will be measured back to you And why do you look at the speck in your brother's eye, but do not consider the plank in your own eye?'*

The sad thing is that we often stop here when we read this Scripture. We need to read verse 5. If we don't, we will think God does not want us to see any faults in anyone. In fact, if we even mention in the right spirit that a particular person may need prayer about something, someone may be quick to say, 'Judge not!' If we don't read the total context of these verses, we are left with the misconception that it is wrong to ever evaluate another person, that it is out of order to ever weigh them; because as surely as we find a speck in his eye, we will have a plank in our eye. Therefore, we could conclude that we are not ever to be concerned about the speck in our brother's eye. We may even think we are doing our brother a service by ignoring it.

Jesus teaches us the proper way to judge:

> *'Hypocrite!* **First** *remove the plank from your own eye, and* **then** *you will see clearly to remove the speck from your brother's eye.'*   (Matthew 7:5)

This passage really came alive to me through the following event:

I had been preaching in a small church in Texas. Some carpentry had been going on in the back of the building, and one of the workers got something in his eye. It was so painful to him. It was only a small splinter, but it felt like a huge rock. People tried to help and he'd say, 'Oh, no, don't bother me. Just leave me alone.' It was a natural reaction because of the pain. I ran to him and pulled out my handkerchief, and said, 'Brother, let me help you.' 'No, no!' he replied. 'Yes, let me help you,' I spoke with authority because that splinter needed to be removed. I opened his eye, and there it was. The splinter wasn't large, but it was dangerous to be in his eye. I couldn't see it too clearly. I was concerned about what might happen if I accidentally pushed it in deeper. We brought him under the light, and I could then see the splinter clearly. It stuck to the handkerchief and I pulled it away. He was so relieved. He grabbed and hugged me, saying, 'Thanks!' While the splinter was in his eye, he didn't want me to bother with it, but when it was out he was very grateful.

Now you are doing your brother a disservice if he is overtaken with a sin and you do not restore him. His spiritual eyesight will be impaired if the sliver in his eye is not removed. But if you don't deal with the timber in your own life, you won't be able to see clearly to remove the speck. In fact, you may even impair his eyesight and cause spiritual damage because you will push that splinter further into his eye.

In order to see clearly we must be able to judge with righteous judgement, which we can do after we've first judged ourselves. This is what Paul said in Galatians 6:1:

> 'Brethren, if a man is overtaken in any trespass, you who are spiritual restore such a one in a spirit of gentleness, considering yourself [as Jesus said, "first remove the

plank from your own eye"], *lest you also be tempted. Bear one another's burdens, and so fulfil the law of Christ.'*

Jesus wants us to take the speck out of our brother's eye, but He doesn't want us to sit in judgement, or we'll only drive it in deeper.

Judge not ... but judge

In 2 Corinthians 5:12, Paul was rebuking those who gloried in appearance and not in heart. We often think, carnal Christians like the Corinthians would glory in appearance, whereas no spiritual man of God could fall into such a mistake.

Let us take a look at 1 Samuel. Here is a spiritual man. Samuel had heard God's voice since childhood. He had received the revelation of God since his childhood. He had judged Israel for forty years, and no record of disobedience or rebellion against God exists in all of Samuel's life. He was a very godly man.

King Saul had been deposed in God's eyes (1 Samuel 16). He was still king but God had refused him. The Lord sent Samuel to the house of Jesse to choose Saul's successor from Jesse's sons. Samuel went; they offered sacrifice; and then Samuel said, 'Jesse, get all of your boys together' (verse 5). Seven of his sons were present. He had eight sons, but he didn't bother to get the youngest. One of the older sons perhaps would be a successor to King Saul but surely not the youngest.

They had been worshipping God, offering sacrifices. The prophet Samuel should have been alert to God's Spirit.

> *'So it was, when they came, that he* [Samuel] *looked at Eliab* [the eldest son], *and said, "Surely the LORD's anointed is before Him!"'*   (1 Samuel 16:6)

This was Samuel's decision. This is the successor for King Saul. This is the next king of Israel. The Lord's anointed.

> *'But the LORD said to Samuel, "Do not look at his appearance or at his physical stature, because I have refused him."'*
> (1 Samuel 16:7)

Even godly people can still judge by appearances. Even godly Samuel, when he looked at Eliab, who was so handsome and strong to look upon, said, 'Surely this is the successor for King Saul. This is the Lord's anointed before Him.'

God had to rebuke experienced Samuel. 'Don't look at his appearance, I have refused him.'

> *'For the LORD does not see as man sees; for man looks at the outward appearance, but the LORD looks at the heart.'*

This, too, is how the accuser comes in. I'm not referring only to the physical appearance of a man, but also to the way a situation can appear. You may hear a story about some minister; the way it appears, you could just jump all over him, but you don't know the full story. You need to pray for God to give you the ability to discern and see what the motives and intents were. Because, while God sees our outward actions, He weighs our actions by our attitude. He judges our methods by our motives. God begins His inspection in the heart.

> *'For the LORD is the God of knowledge; and by Him actions are weighed.'*
> (1 Samuel 2:3)

None of the seven sons of Jesse was chosen by the Lord.

> *'And Samuel said to Jesse, "Are all the young men here?"'*

Because none of these was Saul's successor. Jesse replied,

> ' *"There remains yet the youngest, and there he is, keeping the sheep."* ' (1 Samuel 16:11)

So the youngster was called for.

Along came David. He was ruddy in complexion, and somewhat good to look upon. This was the Lord's anointed. God had to point out to Samuel not to judge by outward appearance. Even a very mature man of God can miss it by judging according to his eyes or his ears.

Pray this prayer with me:

> 'Lord, teach us to overcome fault-finding, grudging, repeating hearsay, and, even if we are repeating what is true, teach us not to do so unless it will bring about good for the Kingdom.
>
> Lord, teach us to dwell on the things mentioned in Philippians 4:8: *"...whatever things are true, whatever things are noble, whatever things are just, whatever things are pure, whatever things are lovely, whatever things are of good report; if there is any virtue and if there is anything praiseworthy – meditate on these things."*
>
> I repent of repeating hearsay.
>
> I repent of gossiping.
>
> I repent of sitting in judgement, faultfinding, and criticism.
>
> I repent of every way that I have allowed Satan to use me to sow discord among other believers. I will no longer tear down my brother or my sister.
>
> I ask forgiveness where I have judged with carnal judgement.
>
> I ask forgiveness for judging men by the flesh, for looking at the outward appearance.
>
> I ask for the ability to judge with righteous judgement, that I will have true discernment and know what is in a man's heart. You alone are their judge.

Help me to build up the body of Christ and grant that I may never again be used as a tool of the accuser of the brethren.

Thank You, Lord.'

Chapter 4

Overcoming Satan
When He Accuses Me to Myself

Conviction and condemnation

Matthew 18:18 is a well-known verse:

> *'Assuredly, I say to you, whatever you shall bind on earth will be bound in heaven, and whatever you loose on earth will be loosed in heaven.'*

The Greek verb tenses are the reverse of the English tenses in the King James Version. A more accurate reading is:

> 'whatever you bind on earth **has been** bound in heaven, and whatever you loose on earth **has already been** loosed in heaven (or "by heaven").'

Let us look at this verse in the light of overcoming the accuser.

The accuser is overcome in heaven even though he still assaults God's people. We can overcome him here on earth because he has already been overcome in heaven. We can bind the accuser when he comes to us with condemnation, with inferiority, or with anything else. We can loose ourselves from the accuser's influence here on earth because we have already been loosed by heaven.

We are to overcome the accuser when he accuses us to ourselves. We need to know the difference between conviction and condemnation. Romans 8:1 reminds us,

> *'There is therefore now no condemnation to those who are in Christ Jesus, who do not walk according to the flesh, but according to the Spirit.'*

As long as you abide in Christ Jesus there is no condemnation. There may be **conviction** but there is no **condemnation**. An illustration follows: when Joshua the high priest was clothed with filthy garments, Satan resisted and accused him (as discussed in chapter 2). The angel of the Lord overcame the devil's condemnation on Joshua's behalf, but after He cleansed him and put new clothes on him and a clean turban on his head, then the angel of the Lord warned Joshua concerning his responsibilities. That is the picture of **conviction**.

There are very definite convictions for those who are in Christ Jesus, but there is no condemnation to those who abide in Christ.

I am not under condemnation. I have passed from death to life. I shall not see condemnatory judgement so long as I abide in Christ.

Conviction may make you miserable – the chastening of the Lord can be a truly sobering thing, but condemnation hinders you from approaching God, whereas conviction will cause you to run towards Him. Condemnation hinders your fellowship with God, whereas conviction will actually aid you in walking with Him. Condemnation looks at your failures as grounds for your having no rights to fellowship with God, whereas conviction looks at your failures and sins as hindrances to your fellowship with God and teaches that the removal of those sins will greatly aid your fellowship with Him.

Many of God's people are experiencing the condemnation of the accuser. They are being accused by the tormentor and are mistaking it for the conviction of the Comforter. There is a vast difference between condemnation and conviction.

But how can we know whether or not we are being convicted by the Lord or condemned by the devil? One great difference is: condemnation is a general, all-around putting-down of the child of God. It comes to you in a general sense. 'You are just a bad Christian. You don't pray enough, read the Word enough, fast enough, or witness enough. You don't have enough love. You don't have enough joy. You don't have enough peace. Look at you. See how those around you do so much better in their walk with God!'

I've prayed for people and asked them, 'What's the problem?'

'I don't know, I'm just bad all round.'

This is what condemnation does: it is an accusation implying that you are just an all round good-for-nothing; that you are the sorriest Christian that ever took the name of Jesus. 'Who are you to raise your hands, and who are you to prophesy when there are other people more spiritual and closer to God than you?' 'Who do you think you are to be used of God?' That is the voice of the accuser.

Conviction is very specific. To follow this line of thought, refer to Psalm 139:23–24:

> *'Search me, O God, and know my heart; try me, and know my anxieties; And see if there is any wicked way in me, and lead me in the way everlasting.'*

I appreciate my background and what I was taught, but I was often under such condemnation, as were most of the people around me. One of our first steps in seeking revival was to gather around the altar. The evangelist would exhort us to 'search our hearts.' When we desperately want to serve the Lord, we tend to look inward; but the inward search is not always the right one.

When you 'search your heart' you will find all kinds of things that will burden you, weigh you down, and bring you low. In fact, you will just want to quit praying. You will get to the point of saying, 'It's impossible. I'll never be what God wants me to be if that is the way it is.' You will throw in the towel.

This was brought to me so forcefully one day when I was reading this Psalm. I realised I had been doing the Holy Spirit's job. In my early Christian life one of the things I would do at the close of the day was endeavour to check where I might have failed God. I would go over the conversations of the day and question, 'Did I really act in love towards those people?' And the devil would say, 'No, you really didn't. You didn't show nearly enough love towards that person. You didn't say what you should have said.' etc.

Then the Lord corrected me with, 'How dare you take My place? You are doing My job. It is My job to keep you in line.'

When the shepherd is tending a flock of sheep, whose job is it to keep the sheep in line? The Lord is my shepherd and His rod and His staff comfort me. When I go a bit crooked, He puts His rod over and gently nudges me back in line. He puts it around my neck, but He doesn't jerk my neck out of place. The psalmist David didn't say, 'Your rod and Your staff torment me.' My Shepherd gently takes me and by His Word and by His Holy Spirit, instructs me in the way that I should go.

David said,

> *'Search me, O God, and know my heart; try me, and know my anxieties; And see if there is any wicked way in me, and lead me in the way everlasting.'*

That is to say, 'God, **You** do the searching. **You** do the looking. **You** see if there is any wicked way in me.'

Now when I come to the close of the day, I'm learning to just open myself up to the Spirit of the Lord and say, 'Lord, You search me – You know me. I'm going to leave all the searching up to You.' This then opens my soul for divine correction, for the Holy Spirit is faithful. When I have stepped out of bounds, it is clear; and when I confess that, no sense of guilt comes, just peace and cleansing. And I'm growing closer to the Lord rather than hanging my head. I've turned the searching over to Him.

Jeremiah 17:10 tells us,

> '*I, the LORD, search the heart, I test the mind . . .*'

We tend to become too inward in our Christian experience. We are like the land of Canaan – a land of many giants, many walls, many cities. When I was saved, I thought that all the old things had passed away and that all things had become new. I thought that was meant for my spirit, soul, and body and didn't realise that it was just in the spiritual realm (2 Corinthians 5:17). Then when something bad came up in my soulish realm, I thought that I needed to be born again, all over again. What I needed was deliverance and sanctification. I praise God that He did not answer my request to reveal to me, immediately and entirely, everything in my soulish nature that needed cleansing and correction.

One evening I got before the Lord and said, 'Lord, I have two or three hours that I'm going to give to You. Will You please tell me anything that is wrong with my life, and let's get rid of it right now.' It must be because of our American way of life that we want 'instant everything.'

A lady once came to me for prayer and said, 'I want everything the Lord has for me, right now!'

'Well then,' I said, 'I can't pray for you.'

'Why not?' she responded, 'I want it all. If there is anything wrong, I want to get rid of it right now.'

I knew where she was coming from – instant coffee,

instant potatoes. Instant ... instant ... instant. We want instant perfection!

It takes many years to grow a tree. It took many years to conquer and possess the land of Canaan. God said, 'I didn't give you all the land of Canaan at one time,

> *'The LORD your God will drive out those nations before you little and little; you will be unable to destroy them at once, lest the beasts of the field become too numerous for you.'*
> (Deuteronomy 7:22)

We have to learn how to go in and conquer and then reign, and then to go in and conquer something else and reign. You don't just go in and conquer everything in one go, you have to learn how to reign over each area that you conquer, otherwise the wild beasts will come again. The Lord said to **conquer** and then **reign**. Don't permit the enemy to point out other walled cities in your life and sidetrack you from **reigning** over one area where God has given you deliverance and victory.

The Holy Spirit convicts in specific areas in which He wants to deal. The time that I asked the Lord to show me everything that was wrong in my life and to take care of them that night, He did show me one particular area of fault in my life. I stayed with Him several hours dealing with it, and when the time was over, the area still wasn't completely gone. The Lord said, 'Don't be impatient. I never get in a hurry. I take just as long as I need to do a work in you. Just rest in Me. Let Me do My work in you.

Many times I see Spirit-baptised Christians who open themselves to the accuser because they are just rushing right in with: 'I want everything God has for me right now; I want to overcome everything.' If they have one little area in their life that doesn't match up, they run for deliverance. We tend to look at deliverance as a means to instant, total perfection. It is not. It is just getting rid of a few giants. There will be more giants later.

'I want to get rid of anything else that I have so I won't have any more demonic problems,' a lady said to me. I understood her plight. I said, 'Sister, there are things in your life that would make you feel just like giving up if God were to reveal their enormity.' God is gracious.

At one point, I thought I was entirely clean; then God showed me terrible pollution. 'Oh God, I didn't know that was there!' I cried. But He knew it all along, and in His merciful kindness He showed me just enough for the two of us to learn how to conquer and reign over one city at a time. City by city, stronghold by stronghold, here a little, and there a little, line upon line, precept upon precept. Stone upon stone.

Condemnation = guilt
Conviction = peace

A second difference between condemnation and conviction is this. When Satan condemns you and you yield to that voice and you confess it to God (for you think it is the Holy Spirit, and you think the Lord is convicting you of something), rather than experiencing relief and peace over what you have confessed, you experience guilt. And more voices begin to speak to you: 'You really shouldn't have done that' and you reply, 'I know, I know.' A vicious cycle begins of confessing that sin over and over, over and over. With each confession of it, you get deeper and deeper into condemnation. Rather than coming out of guilt into peace, you get laden with more and more guilt. When the enemy is condemning you and you are tricked into confessing something over and over to God, you are actually sinning. That is the reason you become more and more laden with guilt. You are calling God a liar. You may be sincere and very well-meaning, but Satan has taken introspection and twisted it, and he has you operating in unbelief. Romans 14:23 tells us, *'Whatever is not from faith is sin.'* By repeatedly confessing a sin, you are telling God that somehow He hasn't forgiven you. He chooses to forget when He forgives. Since you are not operating out of faith, the confession is a sin, and hence the guilt keeps coming back.

During conviction by the Holy Spirit that true voice doesn't go away. David said,

> *'When I kept silent* [about my sin], *my bones grew old through my groaning all the day long.'*   (Psalm 32:3)

God's voice didn't go away. It was persistent, very specific. When sin is confessed, God changes the drought into the moisture of the rain. In other words, great peace and great relief and release come when the yielding is to the true conviction of the Holy Spirit. That 'still small voice' will be known for it does not come with condemning undertones. It comes in a yearning, beseeching tone with, *'Turn, turn from your evil ways'* (Ezekiel 33:11). That is the gracious voice of conviction.

We should praise God for His convicting power in our lives. It is this power that corrects us. God is correcting us when we're beginning to go to the right or to the left. We need to stay on the straight and narrow. If we begin to veer, this gentle voice is heard. The Scripture says,

> *'Your ears shall hear a word behind you, saying, This is the way, walk in it.'*   (Isaiah 30:21)

Condemnation = burden
Conviction = cleansing

A third difference between condemnation and conviction: when Satan condemns the child of God, he does so to rob him of his effectiveness; he does so to kill, to destroy, to burden. When the Holy Spirit convicts, He does so to cleanse, to release, to deliver and to set free.

There is a vast difference in the purpose of conviction and of condemnation.

Satan used to continually bring up my past failures. They would fill me with such regret, with such a sense of shame and remorse. I thought it was good to feel that way, a sign of my repentance. But it was filling me with condemnation, and I was losing faith for God to meet my needs. I did not realize it was the voice of the accuser.

'You remember the time you failed God?' Satan would taunt.

'Remember the time you did that to that brother?'

'What about the time you lost your temper?'

When these accusations came, I would say, 'Yes,' and he'd lay it on me. Talk about a burden! A huge burden of condemnation was upon me. As I continued praying, the Lord said, 'You have yet to realise that when you confess the sin to Me, I not only cleanse and change you, but also I deal with that sin and remove it. I so remove that sin that Satan can never point to it again because it has been dealt with and destroyed.' In the Old Testament the sin offering was burned and reduced to ashes. God said, 'That's all that is left of your sin.' When as a Christian we accept the atoning blood, confess a sin and repent of it, then in the sight of God that sin is no longer; it is reduced to ashes.

When Satan says, 'Look at that sin,' we can answer,

'All I see is a heap of ashes.'

'Don't you remember what you did?'

'No, all I can see is a heap of ashes!' My sin is reduced to ashes!

Ways in which God deals with our sin

I used to find it was easy to say that before I got saved, I used to do this or that. I'd be talking about the most horrible sin and feel no condemnation whatsoever, because all that happened before I got saved. Then some little things that were sins, would bother me continually after I got saved. It was easy to forgive myself for the things I did **before** I was saved, but it was so much harder for me to learn to accept God's forgiveness for the things I did **after** I received Christ.

Many Christians today are looking for an easy way, looking for an excuse to continue to entertain the fleshly life. The message of holiness, which a lukewarm church needs to hear, ought to be preached often. But I am addressing these remarks to people who are sincerely wanting to serve the Lord. They are aware that there are areas in their lives that they have not overcome.

Perhaps you are one of the individuals reading this book whose greatest need is comfort.

> *'Comfort, yes, comfort my people ... Speak comfort to Jerusalem ...'*
> (Isaiah 40:1–2)

If you are endeavouring to serve the Lord, and Satan brings to you little and big things, pointing them out to you after you have repented, haranguing you, I want to comfort you with these words:

> *'I, even I, am He who blots out your transgressions for **My own sake**, and I **will not remember** your sins.'*
> (Isaiah 43:25)

That is to say, it is not your goodness that will effect your forgiveness, but it is 'I, even I. Just because I am who I am.' In showing us His reason for forgiving us, God bases His forgiveness on the merit of His goodness alone. Just because He is who He is, God said, 'I blot out your sin.' For whose sake? Not for our sake, but for **His sake**. Remember David's famous line: *'He restores my soul for His name's sake'*? God does it for His honour. He blots out our transgressions for His own sake. God says to you, 'I have called you by name. You are Mine. I am blotting out your sins for My own honour.' It was this very concept that helped me overcome condemnation. His Holy Spirit continued to tell me, 'I came to you by My free grace. I cleansed you and robed you in My righteousness. I did that for you when you were lost and undone, how much more will I do it for you now that I've called you by **My name**!

That is why David was able to say,

> *'Bless the L*ORD*, O my soul ... who forgives all your iniquities, who heals all your diseases.'* (Psalm 103:2–3)

The Lord heals all the diseases of the soul. He forgives all the iniquities of the soul. The transgression itself is blotted out, and the blotting out substance, praise God, is the precious blood.

We overcome the accuser by the blood of the Lamb and the word of our testimony. We confess the merits of Jesus' blood right back in the face of Satan when he comes to condemn us. We say, 'Praise God, it is written; my transgressions are blotted out.' God has blotted out that sin. Not only has He cleansed and purged me, but that sin isn't what it used to be – it has been blotted out.

In Isaiah 44:22 we read some examples in nature to help us see what God does to our sins. The first to consider is that of a **fog**.

> *'I have blotted out, **like a thick cloud**, your transgressions, and, like a cloud, your sins. Return to me, for I have redeemed you.'*

That's conviction. That is the beauty of the Lord – no matter how we transgress or how we fail God – inwardly or outwardly. God's call to us is always: 'Return to Me. Return to Me.' Condemnation: the voice of the accuser says, 'You are not worthy to go to God. Look what you've done,' but, God says, 'Forget about those transgressions. I have blotted them out. Keep coming to Me. Just keep returning to Me.'

The Lord said, 'View your transgression after you give it to Me as you would something that was on the other side of a thick fog, or a thick cloud.' Well, I've started doing that and it is quite hard to see through a fog!

Yet Satan will tap us on the shoulder and say, 'Hey, can you see way back there through that fog?' 'Well . . . yes.' And we gaze right back, trying to look through that fog at the things that God said to forget.

In Isaiah 43:25 God shows us another aspect of forgiveness. He chooses to forgive our sins, then tells us, *'You will not be forgotten by Me'* (Isaiah 44:21). God deals with us as with children. He willingly forgives our sins. When He forgives, He forgets our sins, but still remembers us. That is the grace of God. It is not so much that God cannot recall our sins, but that He has willingly chosen to forget them forever (Hebrews 10:15–17).

Many of us have been taught that according to the new covenant, God will forgive you; but He is still going to reward you after your iniquities. Psalm 103:10 specifically tells us, *'He hath not dealt with us after our sins; nor rewarded us according to our iniquities.'* God does not reward us according to our iniquities ('Iniquities' generally refer to the sins within us – the inward sins).

God gives us another example from nature that will help us to realize how great His forgiveness is toward His children. This Scripture is found in Psalm 103:12:

> *'As far as the east is from the west, so far has He removed our transgressions from us.'*

The Holy Spirit said something here that undoubtedly David did not fully comprehend when he wrote these words, that is, east and west are an immeasurable distance one from another, whereas north and south are – in terms of the earth – a measurable distance. The Holy Spirit said 'east and west.' Picture your hand as the globe of the earth. There is a North and a South Pole, and an equator. If I say I am going to go south, after I cross the South Pole and come up on the other side, then what direction am I going?

North. When I cross the North Pole the same thing happens, from there on I'm going south. The poles determine that. Had David been speaking from his own mind, it would have been easy for him to say, 'As far as the north is from the south, so far has He removed our transgressions from us.' But the Holy Spirit knew that north and south meet at the poles, but east and west do not. You can go north only halfway around the world. You can go south only halfway around the world. But you can go east all the way around the world and when you get back to where you began, you are still going east. You can go west all the way around the world and, so long as you don't change your course, you are still going west. So, *'as far as the east is from the west'* – an immeasurable distance – *'so far has He removed our transgressions from us.'* Not our transgressions from God, but our transgressions from us. My sins are an immeasurable distance from me!

When I confess sin and repent of it, how dare I let Satan even bring to me the remembrance of that sin, for that sin is as far from me as the east is from the west!

In Micah 7:18–19 we are given another comparison of God's forgiveness to help us realise we can be overcomers.

> *'Who is a God like You, pardoning iniquity and passing over the transgression of the remnant of His heritage? He does not retain His anger forever, because He delights in mercy. He will again have compassion on us, and will subdue our iniquities. You will cast all our sins* **into the depths of the sea.'**

In Micah's day they did not have submarines; they could only go a few feet under the surface of the ocean. Even in our day, the measurement of ocean depths has been changed a number of times.

Not too far under the ocean surface, light disappears, and it is very dark. Mile after mile it is dark, dark, dark.

The next time the devil says, 'Look at your past,' you can tell him, 'I can't see it. It is eight miles deep. It is too far down for me.' Don't endeavour to gaze into your regrettable past. Don't try to gaze at your former sins. They are in the depths of the sea. We always overcome Satan with the Word of God.

In Isaiah 38 we find another picture of what God does with our sins. When King Hezekiah was approached by Isaiah with the words,

> *'Set your house in order, for you shall die and not live.'*
> (Isaiah 38:1)

The king turned his face toward the wall and began to pray to the Lord. The Lord speaks to the prophet Isaiah and again sends him to King Hezekiah with another message: 'Go back and tell him that he will have fifteen years added to his life.'

Hezekiah praised God for the answer of extended life and wrote a short psalm of praise for his deliverance. Notice what he said about his sins:

> *'Indeed it was for my own peace that I had great bitterness; but you have lovingly delivered my soul from the pit of corruption, for You have cast all my sins behind Your back.'*
> (Isaiah 38:17)

The picture here is God taking a sin and slinging it behind His back with the same mighty arm that flung the planets and stars across the sky. With that same out-stretched hand, that mighty hand of deliverance, God has taken all our sins and flung them behind His back.

'Well,' you ask, 'what is so significant about His flinging my sins behind His back?'

> *'God is not a man, that He should lie, nor a son of man, that*

> *He should repent. He has said, and will He not do? Or has*
> *He spoken, and will He not make it good?'*
>
> (Numbers 23:19)

To repent means to look in the other direction. God takes my sins and flings them, or casts them behind His back never to look upon them ever again! He is never going to turn around and look at them. They are behind His back, not before His face.

I don't have to argue with Satan, and I don't have to please him. When he comes with 'You are a dirty, rotten Christian,' I don't have to say, 'But ... but ... but.' Let him think what he wishes. I'll never have to give an account to him. I do not have to please him. I do not have to answer to him. I can be completely silent to his accusations. I confess the merits of Jesus' blood because it is Christ who died, and I'll appear before His judgement seat. It is God who gave Jesus for me, and I'll give an account of myself to God and to Him alone.

When I realise what God does to sin, how He blots it out, removes it from me as far as the east is from the west, plunges it into the depths of the sea, and flings it behind His back, then I should never ever again let the adversary whisper condemnation in my ear over some regrettable thing that I have repented of. Instead, I should look to the merit of Jesus and overcome the accuser by the blood of the Lamb and by the word of my testimony.

Divorce and remarriage

Sometimes situations occur in people's lives that they cannot change. Situations like divorce and remarriage. I meet many Christians who are under condemnation over a mistake they made in the past which is now impossible to correct.

The Bible does not give us many grounds for divorce. I find only two legitimate reasons in the New Testament: adultery and desertion. The adultery has to be a repeated event and not a single act. God requires of you to forgive from your heart that unfaithful partner if he or she sincerely confesses, and then to forget the adultery. (If the adulterers continued on in adultery, according to the law, they were to be stoned to death.) Desertion is named in 1 Corinthians 7:15:

> *'But if the unbeliever departs, let him depart* [if someone deserts their Christian partner]*; a brother or a sister is not under bondage in such cases. But God has called us to peace.'*

As we travel we meet many who have not had sufficient grounds for divorce, and yet they are now divorced and remarried. Some segments of the Church absolutely close any area of responsibility to those in second marriages, even such responsibilities as serving as a janitor or cutting the grass. These same governmental structures, however, will accept the tithes and offerings of such 'second-class Christians.' They can come and sit in the pew, but they cannot serve God within that framework. And these groups feel justified in what they are doing!

In some cases unfaithfulness (a scriptural ground for divorce) has taken place on the part of the Christian. The unfaithfulness is sometimes a cause of the divorce, or sometimes because of pressures that are not apparent. In some instances the whole failure occurred before Jesus came into the picture, and sometimes one or both of the parties is a Christian at the time of the dissolution. Some people point to the book of Ezra, chapter 9, and say that the only solution is for the husband and wife to separate, even though this would cause great pain. Some teach that all unsaved people are in marriages unrecognised by God. I have sought the Lord for answers on this subject, and I believe He has given me a word.

I cannot accept the ever-popular view that heathen marriages are not joined by God. King Herod, who was by no means a righteous person, heard from John the Baptist, *'It is not lawful for you to have your brother's wife'* (Mark 6:18). So God does recognise the marriages of those who are unsaved. God recognised the adultery that Herod was in with the wife of his brother Philip.

I am primarily speaking to those who are bound by feelings of hopeless despair over their past. For example, one divorced man and divorced woman met and later married and had a child. They later were baptised in the Spirit and subsequently came under the teaching that God wanted them to separate. They were greatly bothered by the condemnation that was upon them.

The story of Naaman in 2 Kings will help us to illustrate several principles here, although it has nothing to do with divorce or remarriage. It has to do with idolatry. Naaman, captain of the Syrian army, was a leper who had gone to all the physicians in the land of Syria. He said, 'I need help.' His maid said, 'A prophet lives in Israel. Go and let him pray for you, and you'll get healed of that leprosy.' Leprosy was a fatal disease. He went to the land of Israel, but Elisha, the prophet, didn't even go out to meet him.

Naaman had heard of this prophet and had it all worked out in his mind. 'I thought he would surely come to meet me, strike over the place and decree saying, "Your leprosy is gone." I thought it was going to be like the snap of a finger. Instead he didn't even come out to meet me. He sent a messenger with the instructions: *"Go and dip yourself in the River Jordan seven times." He did, and his skin was restored like that of a little child, and he was clean'* (2 Kings 5:14). In addition to his skin being restored, **Naaman's heart was changed**.

Naaman had been an idolater. None of his Syrian gods had been able to remove the leprosy, but Yahweh, the God of Israel, was able to cleanse his flesh. Naaman was filled with tremendous praise unto God. So much so that he converted to Hebraism in his heart.

> *'Then he returned to the man of God, he and all his aides,*
> *and came and stood before him; and he said, "Indeed, now I*
> *know that there is no God in all the earth, except in Israel;*
> *now therefore, please take a gift from your servant."'*

(2 Kings 5:15)

But, Elisha answered him,

> *'... "As the LORD lives, before whom I stand, I will receive*
> *nothing."'*   (2 Kings 5:16)

Naaman urged him to take it, but Elisha refused. Elisha
wanted Naaman to realise that he could not pay for the
blessing of God, that it was a grace provision of God, and
that he had not earned it in any way.

> *'So Naaman said, "Then, if not, please let your servant be*
> *given two mule-loads of earth; for your servant will no*
> *longer offer either burnt offering or sacrifice to other gods,*
> *but to the LORD."'*   (2 Kings 5:17)

Naaman was converted to the true God. He changed his
religion. He would no longer go back to his king in the land
of Syria and sacrifice to any idol. He was saying, in essence,
'I am never again going to offer any sacrifice to any idol. I
am through with idolatry. I want to serve the Lord **God**.
Would it be all right with Him if I take two mules' burden of
earth from the land of Israel? I want the dirt of Israel. I'm
going to take these loads of dirt back to my country and
build an altar there to Yahweh.'

Because of his healing Naaman was convinced that there
was no other god but the God of Israel. He had tried all the
other gods. Now he said, 'I'm going to serve the Lord.'

Then he remembered, 'Oh, no, this is an impossible
situation.'

Naaman is now going to ask Elisha to give him permis-
sion to do something for which, under the law, he could be

put to death. For him this is an impossible situation. There is no way out.

> *'Yet in this thing may the LORD pardon your servant: when my master goes into the temple of Rimmon to worship there, and he leans on my hand, and I bow down in the temple of Rimmon – when I bow down in the temple of Rimmon, may the LORD please pardon your servant in this thing.'*
>
> (2 Kings 5:18)

Naaman is troubled. He is saying, 'I really believe in the God of Israel and I love the Lord. He is the one who healed me. Rimmon never did a thing for me. But my master requires me to go with him when he worships. When I go with him to the house of Rimmon and he leans on my hand, and I have to bow down before the idol, forgive me.' Deuteronomy 18 says these persons should be put to death if they do such a thing.

Now what is Elisha going to do?

'No, Naaman, you can't do that! It says so in the Word,' Elisha could have easily responded. But God knows that sometimes there are impossible situations.

Listen to this inspired answer of Elisha in verse 19:

> *'Then he said to him, "Go in peace."'*

Elisha's true advice to Naaman would have been condemned according to the letter of the law.

Some people find themselves in second marriages when they begin their walk with God. Because of their desire to serve the Lord, they are willing to do anything. They think of leaving each other and the heartache that would involve. Little children may now have come along the way.

An impossible situation? Something could have happened that from your heart you did not want, but something which, according to the natural and legal limits of life, you must do. How much better is it to rest in Elisha's decree: 'Go in peace.'

'Elisha, are you a true prophet? You've told Naaman to go in peace. Moses taught that to bow down before an idol was an abomination. Are you sure your advice to Naaman is correct?' One may well have asked.

'Yes, that's right. Go in peace,' Elisha may have responded. For couples who find themselves under condemnation and can't go back and unscramble the egg: 'Go in peace.'

Forget the past

When Satan condemns you and accuses you before God, ask these questions:

> *'What then shall we say to these things? If God is for us, who can be against us? He who did not spare His own Son, but delivered Him up for us all, how shall He not with Him also freely give us all things? Who shall bring a charge against God's elect? It is God who justifies. Who is he who condemns?'* (Romans 8:31–34)

When you are under condemnation you need to ask yourself: 'Where is that condemnation coming from?'

Who is he that condemns? It is not Christ.

> *'It is Christ who died, and furthermore is also risen, who is even at the right hand of God, who also makes intercession for us.'* (Romans 8:34)

So if it's not God and not Christ, then who is he that condemns? It is Satan, our adversary.

In my earlier Christian life, I'd say, 'There are several things that I need to do to get to the place I really want to be spiritually. I need to pray more. I need to study more. I need to learn the Word better. I need to become a better witness.'

I've met other Christians who say, 'I have six or seven things to take care of; then I feel I'll be in the place God wants me to be.'

The Apostle Paul said he only had to do **one thing**:

> *'Not that I have already attained, or am already perfected; but I press on, that I may lay hold of that for which Christ Jesus has also laid hold of me. Brethren, I do not count myself to have apprehended; **but one thing I do**, forgetting those things which are behind and reaching forward to those things which are ahead.'*
>
> (Philippians 3:12–13)

The things that are behind are the only things you can forget. Actually Paul does more than one thing: 'I follow after ... I count not ... forgetting those things ... reaching forth ... pressing toward the goal,' but he doesn't even count those as things he has to do. Those things just naturally happen. But one thing he has to consciously practice: forgetting.

We need to learn to forget the regrettable past. Forget, and let the past be put behind you.

Jesus said, *'Remember Lot's wife'* (Luke 17:32). What Lot's wife did was to look back at Sodom. Sodom is a picture of the regrettable past. She couldn't forget Sodom. She had to look back and crystallised into a pillar of salt. Jesus tells us to remember her; He used her as an example. You won't progress in your Christian life if you continue to look at your past.

Jesus gives us another admonition:

> *'No one, having put his hand to the plow, and looking back, is fit for the kingdom of God.'*   (Luke 9:62)

We are not fit for the Kingdom or for the work of the

ministry if we keep looking back. Let the past be the past.

One sister was being prayed for and the Lord said to me: 'She is condemned over the things of her past.' I spoke to her and she began to weep. We rebuked that thing; it came out and she began to rejoice and to praise God. It is so rewarding to see God's people set free from the accuser of the brethren. To be set free from those condemning, accusing spirits that point a finger at us.

All of us are overcome at some time by condemnation, or at least condemnation comes against us. Our only merit to overcoming is the righteousness of Jesus Christ. You'll never measure up enough to please Satan. He will always be saying, 'You could have done this. You could have done that.' But, you **can rely** on the merit of the righteousness of Jesus' blood and overcome by your confession of faith. Join with me in a closing prayer:

> 'Father, I come to You in the mighty name of Jesus. I realise that Satan has come to me as the accuser of the brethren. He accuses me to myself. At times I have been deceived into thinking that it is the voice of Your Spirit, whereas I now understand that the former things are forgotten, and it is Satan who brings my past back to me.
>
> In the mighty name of Jesus, I reject condemnation. I resist the accuser of the brethren. I will no longer allow him to accuse me to myself. I bind his condemning tactics in Jesus' name and will confess the merits of Jesus' blood against his lies. I surrender my will to You, Lord, and believe Your Word of promise.
>
> I purpose in my heart to put a watch over my mouth, to keep my tongue from speaking evil accusations against my fellow believers. I will not bite and devour, but will bless and deliver through words seasoned with grace.

Thank You, Jesus, for Your advocacy at the Father's right hand on my behalf.'

Amen and Amen.

About the author...

David Alsobrook was a minister's son but chose to rebel against the church's teachings at an early age. He studied karate and false religions before committing his life to Jesus Christ at the age of $15\frac{1}{2}$. Before his sixteenth birthday he had read the entire Bible through four times and discovered, to his great joy, that the truths it contained were still in effect and available to believers today.

At the age of $17\frac{1}{2}$ David entered full-time traveling ministry in early 1972 majoring in evangelism and Bible teaching. He has traveled the United States and Canada extensively and has preached in more than 1,200 different places, from jails to country clubs, from a handful of people to thousands at a time. His lovely wife, Ginny, travels with him and sings during the ministry time. The Alsobrooks have witnessed literally hundreds of life-changing miracles in their public ministry.

He has written over forty books, which have been distributed to approximately fifty nations, having been translated in no fewer than fifteen languages. Conservative estimates of his press runs exceed four million copies. Noted leaders of the Christian community have quoted widely from his material in their publications.

The half million copies of his book on abortion, placed in many counseling centers across the US and Canada, has resulted in numerous young mothers deciding to birth their babies rather than go through with their contemplated or planned abortions. People from all walks of life, from prisoners to presidents, have read and commented favorably on his writings and the lives of many people in many parts of the world have been forever changed by the power of the Word of God as testified in the thousands of grateful letters David has received from more than forty nations.

Other books by David Alsobrook

David Alsobrook has authored more than 40 books, most of which are available from:

Sure Word Ministries
PO Box 2305
Brentwood
TN 37024
USA

The most commonly requested titles include:

Learning to Love
Was the Cross Enough?
Divine Energy of the Holy Spirit
The Land of Giants
The Precious Blood
How to Pray Effectively for Your Lost Loved Ones
Awake, Church!
Free from Fear
True Worship
The Seven Temples
Melchizedek: King of Righteousness and Peace

David also has many teaching messages on cassette tape. Write to us for a current price list at the above address or visit our website at:

www.sureword.org

If you have enjoyed this book and would like to help us to send a copy of it and many other titles to needy pastors in the **Third World**, please write for further information or send your gift to:

Sovereign World Trust
PO Box 777, Tonbridge
Kent TN11 0ZS
United Kingdom

or to the **'Sovereign World'** distributor in your country.